MW00805985

So, What's YOUR Story?

Discovering the Story in You

Henry L. Roubicek

Kendall Hunt
publishing company

Online stories from radio broadcasts of *So, What's Your Story?* on KPFT, Houston, and videos of sample stories can be found at:

http://webcom3.grtxle.com/ancillary   Username: Roubicek
                                       Password: Roubicek

Book Team
Chairman and Chief Executive Officer   Mark C. Falb
President and Chief Operating Officer   Chad M. Chandlee
Vice President, Higher Education   David L. Tart
Director of Publishing Partnerships   Paul B. Carty
Product/Development Supervisor   Lynne Rogers
Vice President, Operations   Timothy J. Beitzel
Senior Development Coordinator   Angela M. Willenbring
Permissions Editor   Patricia Schissel
Cover Designer   Heather Richman

Kendall Hunt
publishing company

www.kendallhunt.com
Send all inquiries to:
4050 Westmark Drive
Dubuque, IA 52004-1840

Copyright © 2011, 2015 by Kendall Hunt Publishing Company

ISBN 978-1-4652-6748-1

Printed in the United States of America

DEDICATION

To my wife, Peggy

She never lets me face anything alone

Contents

Chapter 7

Painting the Spoken Picture **89**

Chapter 8

Learning to Tell a Story   **119**

Chapter 9

Working through Apprehension   **137**

Chapter 10
I Heard It through the Radio **151**

Imagine That! **153**
Getting Cozy on the Air **154**

Acknowledgments

Thank you to the UHD students who participated in this project. Without your efforts, this book could not have been completed. In many ways you make my life a perfect story.

Alexandria, Katie, Nicole, Alicia, Kelly, Patricia, Amber, Kirsten, Peggy, Candace, Korlyn, Paula, Chelsea, Margaret, Perla, Cynthia A., Margaret, Ryan, Cynthia P., Martha, Stephen, Dahlia, Mayra, Valerie, Daisy, Michael, Victoria, Erica S., Miguel, Zulara, Erica W., Mitze, David, Esther

Thank you to my friends and colleagues, Jay Stailey and David Rainey for their talent and faith in students.

Thank you to my friends and associates at KPFT 90.1 FM Houston for permission to share so many stories.

Thank you to The Houston Storytellers Guild for their friendship, humor, and place to tell all.

Thank you to friend and media specialist, Albert Holden, for his technical wizardry.

Thank you to friend and photographer, Tom Kilty, for making me look better than I deserve.

Thank you to my family because they are characters more magical than found in any story . . . and *special thanks* to my grandson, Jack, who reminds me why it's important to describe the invisible bird, and to imagine a moving mountain by looking at the motion of the sky.

My grandparents are my greatest source for stories. My grandmother is still the best teller I have ever known. She continues to win the prize.

To Students

The wealth of positive comments made to me by students about their experiences in a storytelling course tells me that you'll probably enjoy it too, but perhaps not for the reason you think. Sure, the subject matter isn't the toughest kid on the block, and that makes its content less intimidating. The real reason, at least for the majority of students, is that this subject may help you to discover why you matter. That may sound far-reaching to you. However, when using stories as a compass, determining why you matter is surprisingly well within your reach.

Curiously, human beings can best detect what matters when they organize experience into story. In her tenderly written *Storycatcher: Making Sense of Our Lives through the Power and Practice of Story*, Christina Baldwin opens with this profound thought:

"Every person is born into life as a blank page, and every person leaves life as a full book. Our lives are our story, and our story is our life."

Your life is a blank canvas, and you have come to this course to continue filling that canvas with your unceasing experiences. You might want to think of this class as an occasion for learning ways to thread together cleverly the feelings, thoughts, and ideas that characterize your life.

I hope this book will help you discover new pathways to storytelling. Many students have told me that they found the first edition of this book readable, meaningful, and painless. That's not bad. Still, I wanted to add descriptors like practical, engaging, and gratifying to the list. I've made some important changes to accomplish this.

Each chapter begins with new story samples; all found on your online supplement, along with a brief remark about the learning principle with which each is associated. You'll be asked to listen, or in some cases watch, some terrific story samples to enrich your overall learning experience. Also, previewing the content in each chapter is in the form of a list simply called, "Understand." Moreover, a set of new exercises are positioned in the text to encourage frequent and meaningful practice. Finally, story excerpts from former students are peppered into your reading to boost your comprehension and improve your storytelling performance.

I think you will open your eyes to a world you always knew was there, yet see things like you've never seen them before.

I hope you become captivated by the boundless energy found in stories. Enjoy!

To Educators

The first edition of *So, What's Your Story?* was anchored by the need to write about storytelling in a human way. As a result, students found it easy to read, and many instructors found it to be the type of text that helped them meet a variety of instructional objectives. This second edition is improved in several ways. Content is arranged so you are able to teach confidently any chapter in any order you wish, creating your own segues and incorporating your own pedagogical style. Like the first edition, I carefully weave theory and practice while infusing even more exercises and examples than before to help demonstrate and support the storytelling principles to which I refer.

Significant content is added in this edition, especially in the areas of personal narratives, methods for learning a story, and in using themes and motifs as practical tools for story preparation. Furthermore, changes made to the online supplement have made this instructional appendage an even more unique feature to this text.

Each chapter begins with a prompt to online story samples taken from the weekly radio show I host. Each sample is carefully selected to parallel one of the learning objectives in the chapter. In addition, I assign an instructional "teaser" to each sample on which learners should focus when listening. All chapters contain two audio samples, except for chapters four and five, which also include video samples of students' stories. In short, I hope this is a meaningful text that doesn't read like a text.

Thank you so much for giving it a try.

As human beings, we become whole by telling and listening to stories. Keep teaching that magic.

To Everyone

Unlike the metamorphosis that occurs to a butterfly or a frog, telling a story will probably not dramatically alter your character, physical structure, or even circumstances. However, as a storyteller, you can imagine it did.

"What's truer than truth? The story."

— Hassidic Wisdom

About the Author

Dr. Henry "Hank" Roubicek is a professor of communication studies at the University of Houston Downtown. Award-winning educator, included several times in *Who's Who Among American College Teachers*, creator and host of *So, What's Your Story?* On Houston's KPFT 90.1 FM, docent at Holocaust Museum Houston, passionate advocate for tolerance education, doggie-lover incarnate, dad to Josh, grandpa to Jack, husband to Peggy, and a friend to everyone he meets. If you ask him his recipe for success, he will tell you *"I have the skills and I might be smart, but what I do best, is everything with heart."* That's his real story and he's sticking to it. Know him for a moment and you will know it is true.

Prologue

I decided to stay with the story I told in the prologue from the first edition. It's not that I'm lazy, it's because it still applies. In fact, thanks to one of the most important principles in storytelling, that no matter how many times you tell the same story, you are always telling that story for the first time, the story makes better sense now than it did before.

Mr. Welch, my seventh grade English teacher, assigned each of us a story to retell in class. These stories came from some anthology, I think. I don't remember the title of my story, but I do remember it was about a young girl, a frog, and a tractor. I know, I know, how could I possibly forget a story with such riveting drama? In any event, I was told to retell this boring story while standing at my desk and, with great poise and conviction, tell the tale to my classmates. I wanted to do well. But how could I? I was a wreck because there were three barriers confronting me. First, my classmates were watching me. I don't know about your junior high experience, but unconditional support for each other was not something our seventh grade English class demonstrated in exemplary fashion. In fact, we hoped each other performed as wretchedly as possible because we figured the more that looked like fools would make the few who did fair look like artistic geniuses. I at least wanted to do fair.

Then there was Mr. Welch. He was actually a very nice man. However, when I was twelve, I thought all teachers were members of the Gestapo. Mr. Welch then was barrier number two, especially when he left his open grade book in front of him while you retold your story, furiously jotting down everything you were doing wrong as you told it. And Mr. Welch wrote a lot. But it was my third barrier that concerned me most. I had to retell this stupid story in front of Brenda Katz, the most beautiful girl in the world. She had dimples, a terrific smile, and no apparent signs of acne. How could

I fail in front of her? Okay, I started to tell the frog story and after a few moments could have croaked myself.

I was beyond awful. I was confused, my voice was monotonous, and my head jerked around as I tried to find a comfortable focal point. I appeared to be lost on a desert, looking for a way out before I dropped dead. I imagined myself continuing to straggle in this wasteland, thwarted by sand and a near comatose state. I had a coarse, dry voice, and I was in desperate need for water, becoming more frantic because there was no water in sight. I stuttered throughout my miserable retelling of the story. I was sweating. My heart raced. I cannot remember if my pulse was rapid or if I had none. I was shaking. The minutes I spent standing felt like a week. I knew the words to the story, but when I panicked, I forgot them. And I panicked during every second of that catastrophic episode. I was the wretched one. The only reason my classmates seemed somewhat sympathetic was that they knew no one could do any worse than I could.

It was clear that consummating my fantasy that Brenda would see me as the eventual man of her dreams had dissipated into thin air. Mr. Welch wrote so much that he needed to take a couple of breaks to stretch and shake his tiring writing hand before continuing on his speedwriting mission. If he graded on points I would have owed him some. I felt my life was shattered.

However, my failure was not the result of any of the previously mentioned barriers. My failure at telling the story well was my entire fault. I allowed my audience, especially Mr. Welch and Brenda, to paralyze me. In addition, I did not know the story. I only knew the words. I thought that would be enough, but it was not even close. I eventually learned that whether I tell a story about myself or a story constructed by another, I must learn to "own" the story by grasping both its content and the ways in which that content should be communicated. I learned that if I thoroughly prepare to tell a story, I could embrace, rather than fear, my audience. I learned to love storytelling.

I just told you a story, one that hopefully kindled some additional interest in storytelling. I know that learning to love to tell stories may not be on your radar. Still, I hope you discover the magic in storytelling. You see, storytelling can enable us mortal souls to make our lives forever remembered by having our treasured stories travel from one generation to the next. Storytelling can empower us to take others on curious expeditions and fantastic voyages to places where imaginary characters inhabit the landscape side by side with humans. Stories take us anywhere we want to go.

I still believe one of the striking motives for telling stories is to make noticeable that invisible sign hanging from our necks that reads, "I matter. I have something to say. I have something to share. I am worth listening to."

I am more convinced than ever before that each of you has something to say and something to share. Say it and share it with a story. Please enjoy your journey.

Chapter 1

The Human Story

Listen to ...

1. **"The Human Spirit"**

   Guest Storyteller: Rabbi Samuel Karff, February 22, 2013

   Listen to the ways in which this teller lets his stories of Messianic Moments unfold effortlessly.

2. **"A Torn Life"**

   Guest Storyteller: Kelli Leng, February 6, 2014

   Listen to this courageous former storytelling student describe her life as one sewn together with solid stitching and put back together with colorful patches and more. This teller fills her story with the kind of emotional shifts that keep listeners on the proverbial edge of their seats. Humor and sadness blend beautifully in this poignant story . . . the kind of narrative that would rival those told by any professional teller.

Understand

Authentic teller
Amplification
Mild exaggeration
Apocryphal story
Personal narratives

*The purpose of a storyteller is not to tell you
How to think, but to give you questions to think about.*

—Brandon Sanderson

Contemplation

My grandmother was the consummate storyteller. Rarely did she engage in dialogue or respond to a question without introducing a story, rich with tradition or wisdom, and oftentimes both, somewhere during the course of the conversation. She would tell the kind of stories one typically finds in the most magical anthology of Eastern European folklore, the kind of stories designed to captivate the senses and heal the soul. Her most intriguing stories, however, were the ones that had no apparent relationship to the inquiry made or to the topic of conversation. For example, when I was twelve years old, I remember telling my grandmother that I was concerned about my future. Then, after her signature smile, she embarked on the story about the mother who took her son to the fair. I glared at her thinking, "What in the world . . . ?" Then she tells the story:

A little boy and his mother attend a fair. The mother won a prize at the fair. It was a sofa. Well, the mother was happy, because she really needed one. She was told that the couch would be delivered in three months. When the young boy heard about the new sofa, he told his mother that he would jump on that couch all day and all night. The mother, becoming a bit upset with her son, told him that he better not. Well, children are children and as children, they like to aggravate their parents, so the little boy continued to tell his mother that he would jump and jump and as hard as he could on that couch. Well, the mother became so angry with her son that she never talked to him again. And the sofa? It never came.

This story may not appear to be worthy of the Pulitzer Prize, but it did something more remarkable: It taught me something. And I remembered it. But what was most remarkable, is that she would construct the story as it unfolded in her mind. She made up the whole thing, right in front of me. The story belonged to her. Sometimes when I asked her a question, in lieu of a story, she would pose a seemingly philosophical remark designed to make a point. I would ask, "Do you like my girlfriend?" She replied, "Well, I'm sure she didn't kill anyone." I just wanted a yes or no. Perplexed, I would ask again, and again she would respond similarly, "I watched her eat and she can use a knife and fork." It was not my grandmother's style to give a simple answer. She wanted me to think. She wanted me to wonder. What she did so beautifully, so naturally, was to use what the late classical rhetorician Carroll Arnold would term a sense of communication, characterized by a communicator's ability to speak with, not at an audience; an ability to share, rather than give information; and ultimately involve, not isolate an audience.

My grandmother's stories certainly made an indelible impression on me. I learned how intelligent she was, and how she grabbed life and shook it by its throat as if to say, "You're not going to get me. I'm stronger than you." The power of those countless unscripted moments was powerful enough to stay with me the rest of my life.

Amplification

Much more famous than my grandmother (although she was pretty popular in my neighborhood) is storyteller incarnate, Joel Ben Izzy. The tales he tells in *The Beggar King and the Secret of Happiness* illustrate the very best of what a teller can offer. One of these terrific qualities is the storyteller's license to create a moral tale to emphasize a character trait. This form of amplification helps the listener or reader to zoom in on the lesson and to understand it more fully and completely. This principle is illustrated in one of my favorite stories, "The Cricket who Jumped over the Moon," found in the abovementioned *Beggar King*:

"Look!" Cricket parents say to their children, "There he is! You can see his face, in the shadows of the moon, watching over us."

In the case of the cricket, the moon is an unlikely goal, to be sure. However, the dream is the central purpose of the story. The magic behind the idea of jumping to the moon is quite fantastic indeed. Nevertheless, are any of us licensed to thwart anyone's dream? This form of amplification is not limited to insects and animals who personify human traits, but in stories about very real people. For example, George Washington did not chop down a cherry tree and say, "I can't tell a lie, Pa." That's right. He did no such thing. Sorry,

I didn't mean to bust your balloons. This apocryphal (doubtful authenticity) story was created by author, Mason Locke Weems, better known as Parson Weems in *A History of the Life and Death, Virtues and Exploits of General George Washington.*

For Weems, the best way to illustrate the impeccable character and honesty of our first President was to do what Izzy does with the Cricket; namely, to design a rich moral tale to emphasize how honest a man served as one of our founding fathers. "This is fraud," you may boldly assert. Relax. Weems is making the point that if Washington were in a position where he had to confess to his father, his compelling honesty would have prompted him to say, "I can't tell a lie. . . ." What makes this case of amplification quite useful in the story is that there is nothing implausible or extraordinary about a boy confessing to have chopped down a tree with his hatchet.

Another type of amplification is mild exaggeration, used by a storyteller to intensify a feeling and make it more pronounced to the audience. If you want examples, search no further than the stories we tell. For instance, consider the liberties we take when we tell about the time when our hearts (pumped a little faster), because the kiss (was a little longer) and the hurt (so much deeper) than in the actual episode. Have you ever added a few more coughs and a degree or two higher in that fever you had?

Just as a quality amplifier in a stereo system can heighten and crystallize the sound of your favorite music, so is the storyteller's ability to amplify key traits and feelings of characters in a story, allowing listeners to obtain a clearer image of the characters. This clearer image helps those listeners become sympathetic for the deserving character, as they intimately and fully connect with the telling relationships between characters in a story, and the lessons that they learn from them. Morcover, since creating magical characters requires that the storyteller maximize his senses to transform beloved characters found in fairy tales, folklore, fantasies, and myths into story characters as real as the people we know in our lives, we will explore how amplification can help paint those magical character personas later in the text.

Amplification is useful when telling any kind of story. The storyteller's license to amplify allows for a greater, more definite set of story images that can grip an audience, and embody the spirit of the tellers themselves.

Or NOT: Disregard Amplification

We know that amplification can be useful when telling an assortment of stories. However, not all stories require amplification. Some personal narratives, for example, are so raw that the story's inherent drama is already unreal. Each of us owns such stories. They spawn from human experiences that trigger our deepest, internal emotions. *War Letters: Extraordinary Correspondence from American Wars*, by Andrew Carroll, is a compilation of letters written by soldiers who collectively fought in a plethora of battles from the Civil to Gulf War. With the rawness to which I refer, a Union soldier writes a letter to his wife, shortly before he engages the Confederate army at Gettysburg:

"My dearest wife, I fear I may not see you again or our darling Sarah. The whole Reb army is waiting up the road I am told and the fragrance of blood, as I write, looms largely and clearly. I long for sleep. Seeking peace in earnest is questioned by most and words are tendered to doubt all but death. I want you, my beloved. I fear the worst, for the worst is to feel fear without the canopy of protection over my heart. I do love you so."

Also in this rich volume are narratives based on the teller's direct observation. To base a narrative on acute observation of an event is an option as equally effective as a narrative about oneself, as well as a potentially powerful form of documentation. Consider this narrative, composed in a letter, by a patron at Ford's Theater on the night of President Lincoln's assassination:

"Wild dreams and real facts are but brothers. This night I have seen the murder of the President of the United States. Early in the evening I went to Ford's Theater. After a little time the President entered—was greeted with cheers. The play went on for about an

hour. Just at the close of an interesting scene a sharp quick report of a pistol was heard and instantly a man jumped from the box in which was the President, to the stage, and rushing across the stage made his escape. This I saw and heard. I sat opposite the President's box. The murderer assassin exclaimed as he leaped 'Sic Sempur Tyannis,' thus always to tyrants."

Storyteller educators have long used *The Diary of Anne Frank* as a source for illustrating how human narratives without amplification can be powerful enough to affect us severely. In *Children in the Holocaust: and World War 2: Their Secret Diaries,* compiled by Laurel Holliday, the familiar tone that laces the Anne Frank entries is felt in hundreds of narratives conveyed by children confronted by their fears and desperation for survival. One young boy at Treblinka death camp writes:

"I was so cold I slept under a corpse. During the night, of course. I didn't realize it. It was very cold and I curled up against someone's back. I slipped my hands under her armpits. I thought she moved. And in the morning, I discovered she was dead."

That young man had no defined audience for his narrative. His letter had "Thoughts to me" written at the top of the page. Communicating a personal narrative to an undefined listener is common practice for those of us who keep diaries or journals. The thoughts we write are in raw form, and can help us to uncover or discover a litany of issues important to us. Those narrative entries we write are truths and feelings we gather and disclose in privacy with our trusting and nonjudgmental friend: the blank book we use for collecting our narratives. We, in fact, become an "open book" cliché. What can we discover about the father who writes this narrative to his son in *Mightier than the Sword,* by Kathleen Adams:

"My dad never yelled at me. But he never told me he loved me either. He never hit me. But he never hugged me, kissed me, told me he was proud of me, went to my little league games, took me trick-or-treating, sang to me, laughed with me. He never talked to me. I can't begrudge the choices he made, no wait, yes I can. What the

hell am I saying? He was miserable. He was benign. But unlike him, I hope I can eventually become that butterfly looking back on my fractured cocoon."

Collecting narratives in journals (discussed later in the text) is one of the best ways to not only garner a deeper understanding of ourselves as human beings with remarkably meaningful stories to share, and keep, but as a way to repair and build relationships with those who matter to us most. Baseball great Mickey Mantle was too late telling his story to his father. Mantle's father died of Hodgkin's disease in 1951. He was angry with his dad, wanted to tell him that he was a terrible parent, and had learned to become a terrible parent to his own children. Mantle blamed this on his father's inability to express love. Truthfully, it isn't important to decide whether Mickey Mantle should blame his father or not. What does matter is that he never talked to his father about the anger he felt toward him. Luckily, Mickey Mantle finally forgave his father after writing a letter to him. However, he wrote that after his father died.

Personal narratives saved by their creators can serve as a magnificent reservoir of stories, not to mention a productive avenue for getting rid of debilitating emotions. However, oral storytellers tell stories. In addition, the stories they tell can work wonders for those of us who are fortunate enough to serve as their audience. Although for most of us an audience suggests more than one person, the best audience is often the audience of one, when stories can work a special kind of magic, as an avenue for heartfelt conversation used to share, validate, repair, and cherish those special moments with the special people in our lives.

The time we take to tell stories are best spent when we are convinced that our lives are worth revealing. I think the best way to ensure that this happens is to take risks, seek challenges, monitor every moment. Look for the good. As for the bad, make them into stories too. Let others feel your strength, courage, and growth.

Become inspired to tell stories by knowing what kind of stories appeal to you. Appreciate how stories make you feel, because the richer the feeling the stronger the identification with the story. Whether it's a folksy little ditty or family story, only you can give your listeners an emotional entry point and permission to feel. You can make the past tense feel present. You can manipulate time, an event, or anything within the context of your story. You are the storyteller.

Final Remarks...

Whether the storyteller creates a tale to encourage reflection, tells a tale seasoned with a touch of amplification, or conveys a tale so raw that it can poignantly stand alone, it is the storyteller's unwavering desire to communicate the story that makes the story, and its teller, inextricably connected. When this connection takes place, the storyteller becomes an agent not of performance, but of authenticity. The authentic storyteller solidifies a relationship with his audience. The result? Every story is real.

"These grandparents were primarily an oral civilization, information being passed through the generations by word of mouth and demonstration, little of it is written down . . . If this information is to be saved at all . . . it must be saved now . . ."

—Eliot Wigginton

Chapter 2

The Power of Story

© Anelina/Shutterstock.com

Listen to ...

1. **"A Lot Learned"**

   Guest Storyteller: Harwood Taylor and Chris Gorman, April 10, 2014

   Listen to these two exceptional tellers from The Moth share two experiences with mesmerizing descriptions, personal revelations, comedic overtones, and heartrending warmth.

2. **"Merging Art"**

   Guest Storyteller: Kapila Love, November 7, 2013

   Listen to the blending of story and song as the powerful duo for this exceptional teller of African folklore.

Understand

Tribal epoch
Oral tradition
Destorification
Learning benefits derived from storytelling
Byproducts of storytelling

"To hell with facts! We need stories."

—Ken Kesey

Of Epoch Proportion

The ninth century fictional storyteller Scheherazade of 1001 Nights saves herself from execution by telling tales. That's a mighty piece of publicity for the power of storytelling, but there wasn't anything else to take its place. Storytelling is all we had. Just talking and listening. No tweeting or texting and forget about Facebook. Before these modern channels gave us the means to document our lives in outrageously exacting ways, we dispatched our personal experiences and family traditions by a whisper in the ear, a gathering around the fire, and congregating in town square. It is likely that storytelling has been around as long as human language. Stories offered the security of explanation, how life and its many forms began and why things happen as they do. When humans engaged in telling each other stories they believed what they heard. They trusted the tales. In short, storytelling is the medium that has dominated longer than any other and humans have benefited greatly from its longevity.

Media theorist Marshall McLuhan claimed that by identifying the dominant media in a society at any given time, the fundamental methods by which a society communicates could be determined. McLuhan would applaud my grandmother, Joel Ben Izzy, and even Mickey Mantle for recognizing the power of face-to-face communication, the mandatory setting for most storytellers. McLuhan cites the tribal epoch (a time marked by an event or by significant developments), with its origins traced as early as 2000 BC, when face-to-face interactions dominated our society. Of course, this is not to say that we have not looked at each other for thousands of years. But sometimes, perhaps more often than we care to admit, meaningful one-to-one encounters are becoming less than common.

Even during the advent of the printing press, when written communication of virtually any type and genre were acccssible to almost the entire population, the time spent by people physically interacting with each other was not tarnished. And today, many of us hunger for the days when our families would congregate for dinner, that daily ritual we followed so that we could spend time together, provide mutual support for each other, and nurture each other.

Because the oral tradition reigned as the dominant media during the tribal epoch, an abundance of stories about histories and traditions were passed along among cultures, helping to cultivate cohesive and independent communities. Despite the tribal epoch having its greatest influence during ancient times, fragments of its distinct oral tradition are seen and absorbed by communities (e.g., Native Americans, African Americans, Italian Americans, Eastern European, Irish Americans, etc.), whose cultures are, and continue to be, largely defined and romanticized by the beautiful stories born from the core of those cultures.

Interpersonal interaction in its purest, most natural form emerged at every turn during this epoch. Communication scholars examine this period to help them rediscover the properties that made conversation so much a part of human experience. Because of their on-going discoveries, scholars have successfully adapted the principles of effective conversation into a working formula for the storyteller: an audience is willing to listen to a storyteller if he can embrace them with knowledge, emotion, eye contact, and passion.

So many current communication channels have either minimized or eclipsed much of our need for face-to-face encounters. How much time do we actually spend listening to and telling stories to our friends? Regardless of the time we might take, it is likely that we spend considerably more time texting, e-mailing, and leaving messages on voice mail. When we throw in virtual settings, it is a wonder that we take time to face each other at all. Certainly, we should fully recognize what technology has done to enhance communication and improve our lives. However, when it comes to telling a story, there is truly no substitute for that live event, when a teller and an audience become a present, dynamic experience.

Destorification

Contemporary writers reinforce McLuhan's earlier insights and concerns. In *The Healing Art of Storytelling,* Richard Stone identifies the term "destorification." He describes this as the growing absence of the need for story in our society. He sees a large part of destorification stemming from the relentless growth of technology in our society that separates people from the need to interact with each other through the telling of stories. Stone's unfortunate conclusion is that without stories, life becomes a book cover without pages—nice to see but not very fulfilling. Vanessa Jackson, President of *Healing Circle,* argues that the spaces for people to tell stories are disappearing. She insists that we must re-introduce opportunities for storytelling in our families, neighborhoods, and even in the international communities. She maintains that the resurrection of storytelling in our society will help us better connect to one another and address deep underlying issues that prevent us from fully healing from many personal events. When you survey some of the material in chapter four, you will learn that the importance of addressing personal events indeed has a direct connection to telling stories as a healing mechanism.

Storytelling is a dynamic experience from which we can benefit greatly. Along with its impact on business, interpersonal relationships, and human healing, the more traditional and proven learning benefits that come from a world committed to storytelling as a prized communication practice are extensive and worthy of discussion.

Learning Benefits

There has been considerable research on ways in which storytelling can benefit us in very significant parts of our lives. To become culturally aware is a great place to start this list of benefits. I have already referred to the relationship between storytelling and culture, because as a method for absorbing the panorama of world cultures, few avenues are as valuable as storytelling. Not only do stories treat us to an understanding and appreciation of the traditions, rituals, customs, ideologies, and practices of world cultures, but also they emerge and shift along with the changing community. There are other appreciable benefits gained by the power of telling and listening to stories, regardless of story type (personal narratives, folklore, fables, fairy tales, myths, and fantasies). Some notable benefits include:

An increased awareness and understanding of culture

A way to better grasp and tolerate different cultures

A way to develop a greater appreciation for the beauty and rhythm of language

A creative way to improve listening skills

A way to refine speaking skills

A way to develop problem-solving skills

A way to cultivate skills and patterns in writing

A way to spark an interest in reading

A practical, fun way to increase vocabulary

A way to develop imagination

A way to tap into your intuition

A way to build relationships between children and adults

A magical way to bring people together and give them a chance to connect

A way to motivate people to focus on things that matter most

At Northwestern University in the 1920s, scholar and ardent lover of storytelling, Winifred Ward, developed a method of telling stories to elementary school students, and following those stories with a creative drama activity. This teaching method is called story dramatization, and it proved to be a powerful tool that nurtures skills such as listening, reading readiness, self-expression, cooperation, and problem-solving, to name a few. In recent years, leaders in elementary education have encouraged teachers to learn story dramatization so they may find ways to teach these skills better to their own young learners.

Beyond those essential skills, this story-powered teaching method has shown to be important in fostering other learning outcomes. For example, one of the elements in story dramatization works to encourage children to use their own dialogue when re-enacting a segment of a story. This single element teaches our children to think about story sequence, and that the thoughts they convey not only matter, but also are vital for completing a task. Recent research reinforces this by pointing to the story structure as naturally leading children to make inferences that are neither terribly easy, nor impossibly difficult. The structure, some suggest, gives learners a reasonable idea of what to expect—a key factor in teaching comprehension.

Storytelling is a communicative art for children and adults alike. Regardless of your age, most people find material presented in a story format more engaging than if it is presented in expository text no matter what the topic. Whatever the communication skill set, and background in delivering and listening to stories, everyone can benefit from experiencing the power of storytelling.

Byproducts

Most storytellers hope that their listeners gain one or more learning benefits. In turn, these benefits can produce equally important byproducts. Byproducts are a set of secondary learning outcomes that come from the teller's unplanned, unanticipated emotional impact felt by an audience. The byproducts from a story will be as unique and as diverse as the complex makeup of most audiences.

Both benefits and byproducts are represented in this narrative told by a friend who recently became an American citizen:

"At the community fair, we're stretched out on a red, white, and blue blanket. It was stained with grass from the time it was pressed against the ground because the seven of us sat there, and we are all heavy people, watching my son's little league game. I didn't completely understand baseball, but I was learning. I smelled something good and was told they were funnel cakes. I knew what hot dogs smelled like and they smelled wonderful. I'm a biologist and know yellow jackets and saw them sneaking around our soda cans. Then it hit me: I'm an American. I just became a citizen. Sitting on that over-worked blanket, 'conspicuously embroidered,' (according to my University of Texas nephew), with American colors, and surrounded by everything American made me feel proud again."

I asked Carl what his purpose was in telling this story. What was it he wanted his audience to reap? He told me he wanted his audience to know him as someone who appreciates the kind of life this country afforded him and his family. What about you? Are there any byproducts for you that came from his story? Do you remember a special Fourth of July picnic? Remember playing center field in little league? Was there too much powdered sugar on your last funnel cake? These possible recollections did not motivate Carl, and none was part of his agenda. However, his story may have reminded you of fond memories which manifested because of his story? Those would be byproducts and can be as meaningful to an audience as the benefits.

Byproducts of storytelling are hardly limited to a single individual. For years, business leaders have known the value of a good story. In fact, many of them believe storytelling will be the most important innovative business skill of the twenty-first century. A quick glance at companies and consultants on the Internet that teach and coach storytelling for a variety of professionals will tell you that the skill of telling is already in high demand. Clergy, teachers, salespeople, and anyone whose job description requires personal interaction all profit from the byproducts that come from a great story. Financial advisors best have stories of success in order to woo potential clients. Advertisers have used stories as their primary weapon for persuading people to make decisions about who they are, what they want, and what they buy.

Narratives are told by trial attorneys to entice jurors and narratives are told by witnesses to form their testimony. Physicians have long known the precious healing that comes to patients who are encouraged to reveal fears about their own illnesses, as well as those suffered by family members. I remember a conversation some ten years ago with a physician friend who died shortly after that talk. She thanked me for the exchange. I wrote about this chat in my journal and this is what she revealed:

I guess my fear around death is isolation, because even though I have all these friends, I know life goes on. I want them to live and have fun but I want them to tell me that I mattered to them; I mean to tell me openly. I know how hard it is to be around somebody who's actively dying. I know how tiring it is, because I've witnessed it as a doctor so many times. I made lots of mistakes. I didn't listen to my patients enough. I treated them like patients not like people who mattered to me.

I gained insight between her physiological and psychological suffering by listening to her carefully, but I think she helped me more than I helped her. I recall thinking, "How remarkable. In her quest to make sense out of life—pondering her own unsettling sense of irony, she seems more grounded now than ever before."

The power of story.

Final Remarks...

Stories produce experiences and experiences leave lasting impressions. Stories go deeper than facts and figures. They offer explanations to things and ideas. Stories shape information into meaning, because listeners experience the immediacy that accompanies a gripping narrative. Storytelling fulfills our needs as human beings. The benefits and byproducts that come from learning to tell stories well number many. The longevity of storytelling as a medium reminds us that our collective urge to tell our tales, from the fantastic and farfetched to the silly and senseless will thankfully endure.

**"We need language to tell us who we are, how we feel,
what we're capable of, to explain the pains
and glory of our existence."
—Maya Angelou**

Chapter 3

Just a Spoon Full of Theory

Listen to ...

1. **"Holiday Stories"**

   Guest Storyteller: Jay Stailey, December 23, 2011

   Listen to the way this teller resonates with listeners through the revival, reconciliation, and reflection of his mother's last Christmas. You will be with Jay in the room in which his mother celebrated.

2. **"Unfolding Naturally"**

   Guest Storyteller: Lacrecia Hinton and Miguel Rodriguez, April 26, 2013

   Listen for the innocence, fear, and raw disclosure offered by these two storytelling student tellers. It's a tale of loss and one of gain.

Understand

Natural storyteller
Testimony
Narrative paradigm
Narrative rationality

"The noblest pleasure is the joy of understanding."

—Leonardo da Vinci

It's all about you. Naturally!

I have had some remarkable storytelling students over the years. Some of those students are able to deposit a wealth of startling information through their recollections, including stories colored with absolute hilarity, and others with inconsolable grief. With her generous permission, I want you to read how one of my students, Peggy, recounts a portion of her life:

"As parents we sometimes give our children those proverbial words of wisdom, which include, 'Sticks and stones may break my bones but words will never hurt me.' Maybe that was my mother's way of pretending that all of the terrible things she called me wasn't that harmful, that somehow I wasn't supposed to hurt. But the words hurt. They hurt every moment of the first seventeen years of my life, when she did not utter one kind, affirming word about me. I remember the time I was waiting for my date to pick me up. I was standing in the kitchen when my mother laughingly commented. . . ."

Peggy, like all humans, is a natural storyteller. This natural process often occurs when we recount experiences and transform them into personal narratives. These personal narratives are an effective, traditional way for people to share, understand, and affirm their ideas, values, and issues. One way a teller can effectively share an experience is seen in Peggy's opening remark to her defined audience, that being how to select a narrative appropriate to the occasion in order to communicate symbolically her message. This example of a meeting with parents is an excellent illustration of how a teller can use the occasion to introduce a story. Whether the occasion is a commencement, eulogy, roast, anniversary, birthday, holiday, or just happy hour, a personal narrative can create a feeling of intimacy and participation for the audience. A word of warning: if the occasion is happy hour, slurring your words will nix the desired effect.

Personal narratives have always reflected the rich cultural and religious heritage of the generations before us, and they lead us to understand how our past has influenced our present. A friend of mine, whose Iroquois ancestry serves as an anchor for most of her stories, often speaks about her family's journey to the northern part of our nation during the late seventeenth century, to what is now Ithaca, New York. Her ancestors were early members in what comprised the oldest living democracy in the world, and illustrates how narratives are rooted in culturally defined scenes, sealed by a flow of behaviors and experiences that provide a meaningful context for the audience.

There are many additional reasons for communicating our personal narratives. Those in the clergy use anecdotes and parables to guide their congregations. Politicians, lawyers, salespeople, motivational speakers all have stories of success, truth, strength, will, heart, and human endurance. Lessons learned from narratives can ignite explosive motivation and can help us to make key decisions and solve complex problems. Those who wish to tell stories about company rituals and corporate stories to a job prospect do so to convey information about the organization's culture.

Those stories told about pep rallies, wartime, past holidays, people missed, boyfriends dumped, Christmases gone badly, times of tears, and moments of laughter during that treasured Thanksgiving when everyone was together were a series of magic carpet rides to each other's hearts. Those memorable stories, frozen in time, can foster the kind of warmth and comfort we tend to find in an old memorabilia box, filled with those heirlooms that validate our lives.

Some scholars view narratives as detailed testimony, designed by a storyteller to capture a group of listeners and give them the detail and incentive to render verdicts about the kind of people we are. Narratives can even serve as ways to get out of trouble, to maintain face, or to protect our dignity. Keeping in mind that we are natural storytellers, consider this narrative from a ten-year-old who wants to skip school today:

"Mommy, I can't go to school today because I threw up all night. You didn't know because I threw up quietly. I didn't want to worry you. And I don't want to give this to anyone, especially Ms. Abrams,

because if she gets sick, then we won't have a real teacher for a long time, and we don't like the substitute. She isn't very good and I won't learn anything. So I better not go to school. You want me to learn things, right?"

Most children of this age have more than likely not been exposed to terms like plot, climax, tone, and coherence, those very terms our English teachers promote so that we can effectively create cogent, detailed, and engaging stories as adults. Since the sample of this ten-year-old's message is a typical, desperate attempt at getting out of school, I sometimes wonder if the story features listed above (those features traditionally and formally taught in school) are somewhat discovered naturally and effortlessly by many ten-year-olds. Children seem to know intuitively the value and payoff that come with a story that makes sense, even when that seemingly sensible story contains fantastic content.

The Narrative Paradigm: Naturally Reinforced

The innate desire of a child to make sense out of the world through story is best explained by narrative theorist Walter Fisher. To Fisher, narration is a "symbolic action, word or deeds that have sequence and meaning for those who live, create, or interpret them." Fisher's notion that humans have a kind of "natural narrative" capacity is worth reflection. However, although Fisher believed that all humans are storytellers, he knew that not all stories are equally compelling. Fisher referred to this as narrative rationality.

For Fisher, two standards are useful for assessing narrative rationality: coherence and fidelity. Coherence refers to whether the story makes sense. Do the events follow each other in some logical fashion? Are there any gaps in time? Is time accounted for? Are things consistent? Are the transitions clear and thorough? How does the story compare to specific stories we are told of similar situations? Are you hearing a story with guided sequence or a meandering maze of confusing details? Look at these two examples of the beginning of the same story. Why does the illustration of the coherent beginning help you follow the story better than the incoherent one?

No suspenders today. I am a model for Calvin Klein underwear. I couldn't wait to get to this reunion. Oh, yeah. Those pants hiked up to my chin. Today I feel proud. No asthmatic inhaler in my front pocket today. I didn't want to go to my last high school reunion because I didn't have any confidence. Those last two years in high school were terrible. Now I do. I was scrawny, and those clips on the suspenders, you know the kind, had those large brass clips holding up my pants. I wasn't exactly athletic. I hadn't yet overcome those laughs. I was never chosen for kick-ball either.

I didn't want to go to my last High School reunion, because I hadn't yet overcome the laughs that came my way every day during my last two years of high school. And considering how I looked, laughs were all I expected. I was scrawny, and needed to wear my pants hiked up to my chin, held firm by those cheap suspenders. You know, the kind, with big brass clips latched on to your pants. Oh, it got worse. I used to carry one of those asthmatic inhalers in my shirt pocket. Needless to say, I wasn't seen as the athletic type. Hey, would you choose me on your kick-ball team? I didn't think so. I lost my confidence at every turn during those years. But today I feel proud. I couldn't wait to attend this reunion. I'm a model for Calvin Klein underwear. Oh, yeah. No suspenders today.

Coherent stories are ones that guide an audience to a desired destination. The stories are fluid, continuous, and listenable. We can follow them. Incoherent stories may make sense to the teller, but they will place the audience in a confusing and frustrating state. In storytelling, as well as for any purposeful form of communication, the audience doesn't just matter, it rules!

Fidelity is the "extent to which a story resonates with listeners' personal experiences and beliefs." Does the story ring true? Are the events in the story somewhat consistent with the experiences in our lives? As a standard for narrative rationality, fidelity can be a bit misleading for two reasons. First, because fidelity cannot succeed by itself. Even when the story theme is meant to resonate with the audience, if the story is not coherent, it will simply take the audience on a fanciful journey into the unknown. Additionally, if those features of presentation and delivery that blend to sing the resonating song of the story to its listeners do not complement the story, the storyteller will most likely convey a message that smacks more of verbal valium, than a story that dances gently and rhythmically on the hearts of the listeners.

The second reason is that a story need not contain a completely consistent and familiar set of life experiences of the target audience for the story to resonate with them. In fact, most stories we enjoy contain characters, plots, and themes very different for our frames of reference. If I successfully tell a story about my grandfather's time in Dachau concentration camp, my audience need not consist of grandchildren of Holocaust survivors for the story to resonate with them. It might resonate with them because they are compassionate. It will resonate because they have a sense of fairness and respect for all humanity. Perhaps they had grandparents who experienced similar plights of atrocity and anguish. Maybe it resonated because it incited them to remember the importance of cherishing our loved ones. Each of these possibilities and so many more could easily ring true for my listeners.

In the film *A Time to Kill*, Matthew McConaughey plays a passionate, fledgling young trial lawyer in the Deep South, defending Samuel L. Jackson for killing one of the perpetrators in the group accused of brutally beating and raping his daughter. This film dramatically illustrates how a story does not need to align with the listeners' set of experiences for it to resonate with them.

The young lawyer's final deliberation to his all-white jury consists of a painfully detailed narrative of the sequence of events leading up to, and including a description of the brutal crime. Before he tells the difficult story, he asks the jurors to close their eyes. After he chronicles the events that surrounded the heinous crime, he pauses briefly and asks, "Now imagine she's white."

Jurors open their eyes. Their collective expressions clearly communicate that the story indeed moved them. Even a jury composed of racists, who would never imagine such a despicable crime leveled at their own children, unless those crimes are committed by the very people for whom they feel disdain, was successfully transported to a place where the pain and anguish they felt for the child had resonated with them. The lawyer's final narrative was not only successful, but was a powerful method for keeping the jurors' prejudice from contaminating the verdict.

Final Remarks...

In a perfect storytelling world, harnessing a story that contains the needed content to mirror your audience would be ideal. Constructing a coherent story that resonates with listeners is a way to make good things happen. Let your passion and your heart guide your delivery. The passion will represent your love for the story. Your heart will show your audience the reason they should love your story. Emerson eloquently sells the marriage of knowledge and heart to a storyteller by referring to the poet: "There are two kinds of poets in the world, the one born of education, the one we respect; and the one born of heart, the one we love."

"Learn to be quiet enough to hear the sound of the genuine within yourself so that you can hear it in the other."

—Marian Wright Edelman

Chapter 4

Yours and Theirs

Listen to ...

1. **"The Richness of Self"**

   Guest Storyteller: David Rainey, September 28, 2012

   Listen to how this reputable actor realizes that storytelling and acting are different, as he relives his sister's death and a puppy's symbolism. This teller is raw, real, and beyond memorable.

2. **"My Dad"**

   Guest Storyteller: Stefani Twyford, May 22, 2014

   Listen to the uncanny color and detail this Houston filmmaker uses to tell the story of her famous photographer father, Martin Elkort . . . a story from black and white turned into living color.

... and Watch

Sample student videos with commentary

Understand

Retrieving memories
Narrative episode
Lifelines
Journals
Difficult stories
Permission
Oral history
StoryCorps
Interviewing
Character

*"If history were taught in the form of stories,
it would never be forgotten."*

— *Rudyard Kipling*

There's Something Happening Here

In her exquisite book, *Storycatcher: Making Sense of Our Lives through the Power and Practice of Story*, Christina Baldwin writes, "Something is happening in the moment. Something is happening in our story and we don't yet know it. We are just in it. We live in story like a fish lives in water. We swim through words and images siphoning story through our minds the way a fish siphons water through its gills."

Because Baldwin's book was published before the debut of the film, *Big Fish,* I found her remarkably insightful and poignant symbolism to be an authoritative, albeit unintentional preview to this delightful film. The movie centers on Edward, a magnificently affable and spirited man whose stock in trade is the tall tale. However, although somewhat amplified (remember that word?) throughout the film, his tales turned out to be not as tall as they first appeared. Edward's tales reflected his colorful range of experiences, which touched the lives of the countless characters who beautifully unfurled in each of his stories.

Edward's son, Will, thought of his father as an unintended fraud whose inflated tales represented his inability to show his authentic self. Because Edward's fragmented life, categorized into memorable episodes, was the story in the film, it was at the end of the story or, with poetic symbolism, at the end of his life, when Will and Edward finally connected. While sitting in his father's hospital room, Edward presses Will to retell the story that he told him many years ago. It was the story about how he (Edward) would die. As a youngster, Edward claimed that he and his friends learned how they were going to die by glaring into the glass eye of one of the most feared witches in Alabama. To appease his father, Will reluctantly agrees to tell the story. As he begins to narrate the story, Will gradually responds to his own telling with a surprising blend of heartrending spirit and gentle, spontaneous laughter, as if he heard the story for the first time. The definition of Edward's life peaked when Will recounts the part of the story when he and his father reached the river. To paraphrase:

I gently carry you from the car to the riverbank, and you wave to the cheers of your loving friends who have congregated there to convey their final farewells to the man they love so dearly. Everyone and I mean everyone was there. And the thing of it is no one looked sad. Everyone was just so happy to see you. Then, I carry you into the river, you hand your ring to Mom who is waiting in the river for us, and I gently place you in the water.

After we see the re-creation of this segment in Will's mind, we return to the hospital room and Will, contentedly reflecting on the end of the story as he smiles, wipes tears from his eyes, and whispers to his father, "You became what you always wanted to be, a big fish." "Exactly," Edward answers softly, and passes peacefully. Moments later, we go to the funeral scene where Will and his wife see the same characters to which his father referred in his stories. Each character is just as his father had painted, only not as fantastic as he (Will) had exaggerated in his own mind, thanks to the fanciful and animated style of his storytelling father.

What do you suppose Will thought as he saw those colorful characters he once saw as his father's delusional formations? What would you feel if you were Will? I'm not sure I can tell you what I might think or feel if I were Will, but I think we might all agree on this: we should have asked Edward more questions rather than draw immediate conclusions.

The stories we tell and the stories we hear should promote more questions than answers. The episodes in the life of Edward Bloom finally helped Will to understand his father. For far too many of us, we take too little time to learn about those we love. Like Edward, we have stories to tell. And like Edward, the stories of our lives are a series of countless episodes, each providing great depth and detail, as well as great lessons of life. Author Barry Lopez says it so well: "The stories that come to us, the stories only we can tell should be given away when they are needed. Sometimes a person needs a story more than food to stay alive. Sometimes when people tell their stories, they brim with bravura. That is why we put these stories in each other's memories." This was not only the case with Edward; it is the case with each of you. So, what's your story?

Discovering You

Rediscovering your life is the best way to find stories to tell. Look around you. What about that watch your grandfather gave you? When was the last time you thought about the hand-made doll made by Grandma? There must be so much meaning behind the charm bracelet, special book, old shirt, series of letters, and old photos. As a storyteller, you invite others into your world by recalling specks, or "episodes" of memorable times in your life. Each of these specks may not have consumed more than a few moments, but when you are able to chisel a chunk of your life into a specific episode, you offer your listeners the richness of depth and the gift of clarity. As a result, listeners will not only become more interested in your story, they will become a part of your story. Notice the depth and focus in the following segment from a personal narrative delivered by the suffering young man.

"Every morning it's the same thing. I get into the shower, left foot first, and then scrub my right arm sixty-four times, not sixty-three or sixty-five, but sixty-four times. My left arm gets scrubbed only thirty times because it is cleaner. Washing my hair takes an hour. I would wash the back of my hair, the sides of my hair, the front of my hair, and the very top of my hair exactly in that order and, as you may have guessed, each part will receive exactly fifteen minutes. When I am finished with my hair, I wrap the soap around my neck at least fifty times. I would continue this way . . ."

Rather than sharing a grocery list of daily tasks that describe nothing more than the crust that surrounds the forces behind this debilitating disorder, this young man took a concentrated approach. It is the denseness with which he tells the painstaking event that gives his listeners an acute understanding of how he copes with a ritual most take for granted.

Consider how a focused narrative conveys the most complete parts of us. If you were this young man and given five minutes to describe the agony of your disorder, would you choose to take your listeners into your world by telling them the story about your two-hour shower, or about as many agonizing rituals that you can cover in five minutes? Does someone have to know everything about you in order to know something significant about you? Sometimes the more we know about a person, the less we know about that person. A focused episode, that mere speck, allows a storyteller to carry a bundle of emotions with him, and sprinkle those emotions on the listeners as he sees fit.

Episodes

I have mentioned the term, narrative, a number of times. So before we go any further, let's make the concept clear. A narrative is some kind of retelling, often in words, of something that happened. The "something that happened" element is the story. The retelling can be spoken or written, but until the story is retold, it is not a narrative. A story is a sequence of events and a narrative recounts those events. In short, to say "Tell me a story" is technically incorrect. "Tell me a narrative" is more precise. Narratives can be personal or stories written or handed down by others, then told again by you. Telling the story of Cinderella is a narrative. Similarly, telling the story of your first birthday party is a personal narrative. A narrative account is made up of episodes. Let's explore further the analogy between a personal narrative and an episode.

Imagine your life as a drama or sitcom televised each week. Each week your audience is exposed to an episode that focused on a densely detailed segment in your very comprehensive life. The episode might be about an argument you had with your best friend. Maybe it's about a sleepover or the night you camped out in the backyard and thought you saw aliens from outer space. Maybe the episode is all about your first kiss. It was that kiss on the front porch of Sally's house, when her father came out at the wrong time for you, but right time for him. How about the first day you brought home your beagle puppy, Buster? What do you mean your teacher didn't believe you when you had laryngitis the day you were to give your speech? Think about the time when you and your friend, Milton, had on the exact stupid-looking shirt when you met him at that disco in 1976. The fact that neither of you were going to pick up girls wearing the same hideous polyester shirts (that was a fact) would be a great story. In next week's episode, you can tell us about the time your polyester shirt caught on fire because you stood too close to the old-fashioned stand-alone heater. What did you expect? You were wearing molecules. I think we have talked enough about episodes. Besides, I can always do another episode about episodes in the next edition.

Now let's talk about other ways to generate ideas for your narratives. Ask yourself questions to rediscover your life and collect some solid answers to help you construct your stories. Find out who and what has dotted your personal landscape. Acquire a sense of inquiry. Here are some suggestions:

Choose a family heirloom or artifact. Where did it come from? How old is it? How did your family value it? Who has it now? What will happen to it in the future?

Describe your hometown. What type of people lived there? Who lives there now? How do you remember it? Describe your school. Was there a teacher who stood out?

Describe your relationships with grandparents or elders. What effect did they have on you? What kind of conversations did you have or might like to have with these people?

What do you know about the origins of your family? Is your family history recorded somewhere? Ask your older sibling what it was like at home before you were born.

What is the origin of your name? Were you named after someone? Were any of the names of your ancestors changed when they came to this country? What is the connection between your name and ethnicity, religion, or culture? Why do you have the nickname you do?

What mysteries or skeletons remain in your family's closet? What languages were spoken in your home? What kinds of music or art were you exposed to growing up?

Who is the keeper of the flame in your life? Whom do you wish to most emulate?

What kind of celebrations did you have in your home growing up? What were your favorite foods?

What kind of letters would you want to write to family and friends?

What are some things for which you want to be forgiven? Why is it difficult for you to forgive?

Do you have a Rosebud, like in *Citizen Kane*? You never saw *Citizen Kane*? Rent it and watch it yesterday.

I know you get the idea. This kind of list of questions is limited only by your lack of interest, inquiry, and imagination. What you will also find is how helpful these questions can be when exploring ways to begin your stories. How could that doctor tell you that you have the chicken pox the day before you planned to go to the opening game of the World Series? How did you feel the moment your best friend told you that she has cancer? What prompted you to tell the officer that you did not see the speed trap? Did the word "trap" mean anything to you? You were watching a western on television and you suddenly had aspirations about becoming a sheriff. What picture came to mind?

I was walking down a dusty street on a cloud-enshrouded night, ready to outdraw and kill five of the most ruthless outlaws in the west who were waiting to ambush me just as I reached the shadow beneath the street lamp in front of the general store. Suddenly, "Boom . . . pow, pow, pow." I got 'em. Yes. I was the hero. I got pats on the back, free drinks at the saloon, became sheriff, and won the heart of the preacher's daughter all on the same day.

Tell us about that fantasy (and fill it in some), that wonderful story that would otherwise remain trapped in your mind desperately wanting to come out.

Reflective questions can be enormously useful in helping you to identify the contexts in which story-worthy episodes occurred. When do you feel the saddest or happiest? When do you feel the safest? When were you most embarrassed? Do you remember the best conversation you ever had? Who gave out the best candy on Halloween? Why do I feel so excited when I think of myself as a storyteller? You want to leave that one out? Nah!

Before I continue to show you how you are someone with a very deep well of stories, I would like to offer this short list of movies (random order) marked by a core of well-constructed and captivating personal narratives found within each film. Watch some of these films. They will serve as entertaining examples of compelling stories, as well as creative thought starters for your own narratives. I'm sure you can think of many other movies that contain some noteworthy narratives. Jot them down and fill the list. What makes the narratives in those movies work for you? How will they help you form your own narratives?

Little Miss Sunshine	Other Movies with Narratives. List Them:
The Big Chill	
Kramer vs. Kramer	
I Never Sang for My Father	
Father of the Bride (1950)	
The Godfather	
Little Big Man	
Life is Beautiful	

Music Box
My Dog Skip
Fly Away Home
The Green Mile
Dead Poets Society
Paper Moon
Liar Liar
Unstrung Heroes
On Golden Pond
Nothing in Common
American Beauty
To Kill a Mockingbird
Mrs. Doubtfire
Stand By Me
Field of Dreams
Little Voice
Life as a House
Vertigo
Rear Window
Gentleman's Agreement
Broken Embraces
October Sky
Philadelphia
Notebook
The Apostle
Walk the Line
Nebraska
Dallas Buyer's Club
Blue Jasmine
Midnight in Paris
In America
Million Dollar Baby
The Pianist
The Emperor's Club
Lincoln
Shipping News

Now back to you.

Permission to Tell Difficult Narratives

The list of films has something else in common, that being they center on difficult story themes. Like the stories that drive these films, many of your personal narratives will reveal difficult moments; so consider some helpful insights offered by Elizabeth Ellis in her book *Inviting the Wolf In.* She recommends you ask yourself some fundamental questions about permission: Have you given yourself permission to tell the story? Have you accepted the risk that your listeners may view you differently if they hear this story? Do you have the permission of the other people in the story to tell this story about them? If not, are you willing and able to make sufficient changes in the story to protect their character, identity, and dignity? Have you prepared your listener to hear the story?

Your honesty as a teller is determined by how prepared you are to enter the story. Only then can you expect your audience to fully enter the story you will tell. Ownership, another essential variable for telling a difficult story, means you have internalized the tale. You are comfortable with it, as it has passed from a thing you once memorized to something you can now convey in your words and be faithful to the spirit of the story. Permission, to a storyteller, is the stuff of honesty and ownership. It is a formula that commonly produces the confidence needed to share difficult and sensitive narratives.

For a long time Kelly didn't give herself permission to tell the story about her abuse. Once she did, she was able to absorb the squirming of many of her listeners. I watched her. She paused and smiled at her listeners. She let them squirm in their seats. She waited until all eyes were on her. She knew what she needed to accomplish. She acted confident and we felt it. Here is an excerpt of the story she told.

... "I drove and ended up buying a puppy. I wanted to love something that loved me back. He broke down my door. He hated that I had a puppy. He said he couldn't have me love anything more than I loved him. I can't tell you what he did to my puppy because if I do I will need to be locked in an asylum. Please don't ask me. Just don't..."

For over two years she wanted to tell that story because she knew many women needed to hear it. She was right. But Kelly needed to give herself permission first. Her audience knew it was worth the wait.

Your Lifeline Is a Road to Self-Discovery

As another method, I have my students do a lifeline exercise to help them determine a possible topic for their personal narratives. I ask that they draw a line on a sheet of paper. Then, they take five minutes to think about significant events in their lives. I make it clear that determining whether these events made a positive, negative, or even little impact is not yet important. What is important is to identify those events, people, or things that, for some (known or unknown) reason, immediately come to mind.

I ask them to consider these events in chronological order and show that order on the line. When it is time to place these "memories" on the lifeline, I encourage them to label the events as positive, negative, or neutral to determine their vertical placement on the lifeline, and to indicate them with some icon (e.g., word, date, picture, etc.) that will prompt their memories. For example, if your stolen bicycle and death of your grandmother both came to mind when reflecting upon significant events in your life, and if your stolen bike preceded the death of your grandmother, as well as being less significant (but still sad), your perspective, illustrated on your lifeline, might look like this:

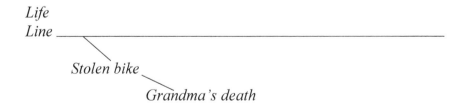

*Life
Line*

Stolen bike

Grandma's death

The same is true for positive memories:

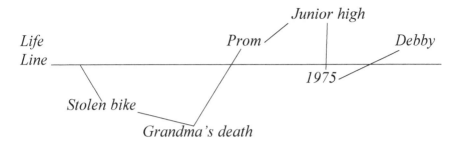

The next set of instructions is especially important. I tell my students that the memories they choose and eventually display on their lifelines are not memories they will be forced to share with anyone. What does matter is that they choose the memories that come to mind within the given five-minute period. After everyone completes their lifeline, I make it clear that although this is a simulation (that it would take far longer than five minutes to sift through significant life memories), the exercise affords them the opportunity to determine which memories are narrative-friendly and which are off-limits (disclosure must be comfortable and regulated by the teller).

I break them into pairs and ask that they talk about those memories that might ignite a possible narrative. Each pair discusses comfortable ways to transform a memory into a narrative. With the permission of one of my former students, Alicia, here is an example of a segment from her narrative, born from the lifeline exercise:

"My Dad knows I love him. Still, I wish I was more comfortable in saying those words. Those were my thoughts on the day I stuck my tongue out at my dad. But the last laugh was on me. As I stuck out my tongue, teasing him, and in a way, thanking him for the silly clown-like behavior he exhibited in front of my friend and me during a beautiful morning walk in the park, I walked toward a banana peel lying on the ground, clearly discarded by some irresponsible person. So, as I walked away, I slid on the errant peel, falling like a clumsy comedic actor trying to get a laugh. I wasn't

hurt, but my Dad came running to me as if I were tragically wounded. As I lay on the ground looking up at him, I saw his eyes, filled with fear and love, and I thought, 'My Dad is crying, because I slipped on a banana peel?' Then suddenly I said, "I love you Daddy."

Using the lifeline exercise to track your life can be a helpful way for generating ideas for stories about your life. A lifeline can drive you to the highs and lows of your most significant moments, and afford you the chance to identify those moments worthy of moving reflection.

"Tracks of My Tears ..."

Speaking of tracking your life, I bet many of you keep diaries or journals. There are many excellent reasons to keep a journal, not the least of which is to document and validate your life. With pen and paper (preferably a blank book), you can take time to explore your feelings and express your deepest desires.

As argued in the January/February 1991 issue of *American Health*, the act of writing a journal can be an avenue to that interior place where, free of pain and doubt, we can confront traumas, put them to rest, and heal both body and mind. Journal entries should be written in raw form, with no spell checks, grammatical concerns, or proofreading. In fact, there should be little thought to the composition of an entry. If we are angry, we can say (write) what we want. We can push hard on our pens and even clench our jaws while writing. Alternatively, we can laugh aloud when writing about something so incredibly wonderful and funny that the act of writing about it compels us to internally reconstruct it, and again respond actively to it. When we date our entries, write the time we wrote them, and sign them, they become even more disclosing and meaningful.

Keep your journals private. They are yours and yours alone. The words you write can have healing power even if you are the only one who will ever read them. The ostensible meandering and disconnecting thoughts that are characteristic of many journal entries are seen in Michael Blumenthal's personal reflection in *All My Mothers and Fathers*:

"I love my son. I need, but perhaps do not quite know how to love, my wife. I long for my lover's singing and resonant flesh in the late afternoons. I want the securities of socialism but the consoling, though somehow often illusory, choices of capitalism as well . . ."

These oblique deliberations were a product of Blumenthal's on-going attempt at trying to put his life back together after learning that his mother, who died of breast cancer, was not his biological mother. What do socialism, love for his son, perplexing love for his wife, and longing for flesh and song have to do with his mother? Only he has to know. Still, as this wonderful book unfolds, the reader finds an amazing connection between the tortuous feelings he shares and the ways in which he reconciles himself for not knowing the identity of his mother until years after her death. Once the reader experiences the winding thoughts of the author, he provides refined interpretations of those thoughts, and those very thoughts then become clear to the reader.

Refining the interpretations of your journal entries can become some of the best sources for personal narratives. When we choose to refine some of our entries and transform them into personal narratives, we intensify our ownership of those stories, producing an astounding level of self-confidence. Cynthia delivered a riveting personal narrative, doused with ownership and confidence that spawned from one of her more difficult journal entries. With permission from this courageous student, here is a segment from her narrative:

"I guess her last days . . . the days when she was conscious, were the hardest. Her bed was downstairs to make it easier for family and friends to visit her. I remember one morning; early morning . . . very early in the morning, my great aunt came over along with some cousins. You know what my mother asked me to do? She told me to make some coffee, because no one probably had breakfast. I looked at her. Coffee? You want me to make coffee? I did but I hated it. I

was mad at my relatives for being alive and being able to drink coffee. I was angry with my mother too. I couldn't believe she wanted me to make coffee, because I wanted to spend every moment with her. I made coffee. The dog howled. I went back into the room. My mother was dead. I think she waited until I left the room to die. I have spent eight years thinking about that day, that moment. I think about it every night. I don't know what to do with it. But I can't let it go."

Cynthia's confidence was largely a product of being able to distinguish between what she felt and why she felt it. At the time she told the story, she still struggled with the "why?" Still, she had control of the story. It was hers. She told me that her journal served as a great source for several of her narratives.

What you write in your journal depends on your circumstances. Entries can range from thrilling to boring events, sad to happy moments, and situations that were peaceful and others traumatic. Coping with death, divorce, or some other major event will not make you instantly feel better after writing about it, but it will allow you the chance to revisit the event and learn from it. Because all stories have a feature of tension or conflict in them, writing it down also means you are not denying the difficult nature of the event or the tension that surrounded it. You do not want to hold on to the conflict, and writing it out allows you to let go of debilitating emotions such as rage, bitterness, and hatred. Feelings that come from thoughts that are free and clear can stimulate great ideas for narratives.

Keeping a journal can serve as a constant and productive reminder that none of us should view any day in our lives as empty and aimless, but rather what George Orwell believed about personal journaling: "It sets me apart from the anonymous mass." Moreover, learning to build a potentially rich reservoir of narratives by writing about our rights and wrongs, highs and lows, and strengths and limitations is a precious reliquary; like a light that passed through a prism and arms us with optimism and hope. Memorable storytellers tell stories of hope and optimism so that the stories themselves can continue to live and breathe forever.

Prompts for Practice

Here are a few thought-starters that may serve useful to you. Choose one, take a couple of minutes to think about it, and give it a shot.

A day that stands out

If I had a million dollars to give away

If cats/dogs ruled the world

A trip to remember

My favorite day of the year

If I could only eat three foods forever

Why books are important

Three surprising facts about me

How to impress your parents

A job I'd love to have

If I could have dinner with anyone

If I could travel through time

Three things I'd change if I ruled the world

The more we communicate, the less we really say

When I grow up . . .

A difficult moment

A joyous moment

A spiritual moment

Memorable experience with nature

Something of which I am most proud

A Great Conversation

Clearly you noticed that some of the abovementioned sample narratives were about other people in the teller's lives. Those "others" deserve special attention because they can create a new and exciting storytelling experience for the one about whom the tale was crafted, as well as the teller and his listeners. Leading the kind of conversation needed to ascertain the tender disclosure offered by the story's central character can be one of the most rewarding encounters you can have.

Remember that favorite conversation? You sat there, sipping coffee while listening to the person seated across from you. You never once looked at your wristwatch. You weren't impatient during that long pause. You didn't become restless at the thought of the story going a bit too long. You were captivated by the telling. If you asked questions you asked them after you heard something about which you needed clarification or elaboration. Assuming you have permission from the teller, this is a story worth remembering and ultimately sharing with listeners. It's a story about someone else, a story recounted in a spellbinding fashion. Those stories about you we surveyed in the first part of this chapter certainly consist of additional characters, each with their own eccentricities. Nevertheless, telling a story about someone else exclusively can be as intriguing and essential as stories that focus on you.

And when we tell stories about others, they often unfold into oral histories, one of the most significant ventures in which we can become engaged. Their stories remind us that we all matter. We are reminded of how we've touched the lives of others, and we let the other person know that he will not soon be forgotten. Stories we extract from others can prove transformative as well, because they remind us that contrary to what we might deduce from establishments which tend to underestimate the vulnerability of human feelings, that we are defined by our character, courage, and heart. However, unlike narratives told with a dousing of amplification, these oral histories must be saturated with accuracy. A glance at StoryCorps and a quick inspection of the appropriate interviewing skills required by the one obtaining the history can help us to better understand the difference.

StoryCorps

Although there are several models of ways to document the lives of others through stories, few storytelling initiatives deserve more respect than the StoryCorps mission. It was launched in 2003 at Grand Central Station, as a national initiative to document everyday history through the unique stories of America as told by common people. It's easy to participate. You make an appointment to visit one of the recording booths. Bring anyone you wish to interview. A StoryCorps facilitator meets you. Then, you enter the booth, record your interview, and two broadcast ready CD's are created: One goes home with you; the other goes into the archives. StoryCorps travels across the country to record, so go to storycorps.org to get their schedule. Conducting an oral history project is an excellent way to learn about the magic of human documentation. To conduct it effectively requires a working understanding of how to wield a few basic communication tools. Here are some recommendations if you are interested in conducting your own oral history project about someone else.

Someone Else's History

Your first step is to learn as much as you can about the subject. Discover as much as you can about the person from primary and secondary sources, historical accounts, network associations, church, school, hang-out places, and more. Try to discover what realms of experience seem important to the person you wish to discover. The richer your background knowledge is, the richer your interview will be. Next, plan some questions. Carefully define the broad historical questions you wish to address in the interview. Ask yourself the "so what" questions: why is it important to know this? What can I learn from interviews that I cannot learn from other sources? Develop a list of interview questions with possible subtopics under each. You will likely be revising those questions as you learn more about the subject as well as your interview style.

Before you interview the person, have a pre-interview conversation so you can explain your reasons for the interview, answer any questions your interviewee might have, and describe how the information will be used. Most important, a pre-interview session will give you the chance to establish a supportive climate, one that yields trust and openness. Perhaps you'll want to conduct your interview using a chronological "life story" approach, or focus on one or a few specific themes: childhood games, school life, work and migration, traditions and customs, food, courtship and marriage, dreams, times of despair, and so on.

The word "interview" means viewing internally. Consequently, be sensitive to your respondent's comfort levels with certain questions. Ask your subject for permission to have the interview recorded. What I say to my interviewees is "I want to be sure that the things we discuss and the thoughts you share are untainted." I also ask them for permission to tell their stories as part of my storytelling repertoire, just like students who gave me their permission to tell you their stories in this book. Consider the style of questions you will use. Open questions, those that give a respondent considerable freedom to answer many ways, are effective if the respondent is comfortable with the topic. Closed questions, ones that are restrictive in nature and limits the answer options available to a respondent, might be a better choice for interviewees that are initially shy or reticent.

Orchestrating an interview can be challenging so be patient. Show signs that you are listening by issuing meaningful probes, allowing for pauses and moments of silence, and by rendering gestures of encouragement and support. Try to omit clichés such as "I know how you feel," and use statements like, "That had to be painful, "I can't believe you were strong enough to handle that," and "This is captivating. Please tell me more." These don't sound like questions, you say? All good questions don't sound like questions. Because they demonstrate active listening, direct statements oftentimes convey an interviewer's intense degree of engagement more than a standard question. Here is a list of questions that most respondents find comfortable, creative, and meaningful.

Generic set

What have you learned in life?

What does the future hold?

What makes you most proud?

Do you have any regrets?

What was the happiest (saddest) moment you ever spent?

Tell me something about you no one else knows.

How do you want to be remembered?

Content and person specific

Describe what it was like growing up in your neighborhood.

Tell me everything you remember about your room in your home growing up.

Who was your first true friend?

If you could choose your siblings, would you choose the ones you have?

Tell me the best thing your mother baked.

Describe your favorite birthday.

Who in your family was your hero?

What is your favorite childhood memory?

How much can you tell me about your ancestors?

In addition, documentation and dissemination are issues you'll want to consider. While not a substitute for listening to the voice of the interviewee, transcriptions are useful for quick access. However, transcribing is very time-consuming. Perhaps you will want to transcribe selected, notable portions of the interview? If the interview was conducted in a language other than English, you may also consider translating into English so that you can share it with more people. To maximize your audience, post the audio on your blog or personal website, along with information about your project objectives. Include your personal comments on the interview process and what you learned from the experience.

Considering Character

Seeking stories from others about themselves forces us to listen closely to one another. The stories we hear helps illuminate the true character of someone. Enjoy these paraphrased segments given by two StoryCorps interviewees sharing their stories documented in *Listening Is an Act of Love: A Celebration of American Life from the StoryCorps Project*, edited by Dave Isay. What do these narratives tell you about the character of those telling their stories?

I love my passengers. I remember one woman in particular, a senior who had gotten on my bus. She seemed completely lost. I asked her if she was alright. She said she was looking for a restaurant . . . the one in which she was meeting friends. I asked a gentleman, a passenger, if he would be kind enough to give the woman his seat so she could sit near me. I was worried about her. I told the few passengers on the bus that I would return in a few moments, that I was going to try to find the restaurant for the elderly woman. I found it. Three animated women came out of one of the establishments looking for someone and I sensed they were the friends she was supposed to meet. I ran back on my bus and said to her, "Sweetie, your restaurant is right here. Let me kneel the bus." Kneeling the bus means I bring it closer to the ground so she can exit easier. I wanted to make her feel special, like it was sort of a limousine. She turned to me and said, "I've been diagnosed with cancer, but today is the best day of my life." I never forgot that woman. She's a cancer patient and because I helped her find her friends and helped her off the bus, she said she felt like Cinderella. It just can't get better than that. I know, I'm a bus driver. I'm not that smart, educated, or rich. But you know what? That was the best day of my life too. **Ronald Ruiz, New York City, July 2008**

Even when I was in basic training, I felt a cloud over my head. I knew a lot of guys that got drafted would go to Vietnam, and it was a kind of darkness waiting for us. I went. Let's just say that and keep it there. I went. When I got back, I didn't shave or cut my hair or anything. I didn't feel like it. I decided to take a long bike ride. I rode straight north through Minnesota. Then, I cut over and headed west. I went all the way to Vancouver. It took me six weeks. It helped a lot, you know, the healing . . . One day suddenly something broke. And I cried. I sobbed like a baby. I sobbed for weeks. I couldn't stop. I still sob. **Tom Geerdes, Murray, Kentucky, October, 2005**

Pair up with a classmate. Decide on one of these topics: Your best day or your worst day. Take five minutes to interview each other, and be sure to do it one at a time. Take notes. When you have completed the interviews, take an additional five minutes and plan a retelling of your respondent's story. Note how I am phrasing this: Retelling, not summarizing or synthesizing. Make choices about the part or parts on which you want to focus. Imagine yourself reflecting back on this session with fond memories. Prepare a two-minute retelling to be conveyed in narrative form to the class. Here is an example of how it should be framed:

Harry told about that day, that awful day when he came home and was told his dad lost his job. At first he was angry . . . at someone, but then realized he was angry because he might not be able to go to the college he planned to attend. It was expensive and . . .

Betty never imagined that a typical Thursday, March 17, 2011, would be the day she met the true love of her life . . .

If either of you find that telling the class is an invasion of personal privacy, then simply retell the story to your partner. Enjoy your short interview. Take it seriously and get a feel for the difference between respondents telling their own stories and interviewers telling the stories they heard. Whether their story is told by them or by you, the outcome produces an historical piece of information about the core of a human life.

Final Remarks...

Like every human being, you are a storyteller by birthright. Each of you is born with an endless supply of personal and universal themes. Open yourself up to the wealth of stories that mold your life. Like self-discovery, learning the story of another person is an extraordinary happening, and one that makes the person charged with extracting that story responsible, in part, for sustaining the history of humankind. Regardless of whether it's a story about you or a story about them, if it's a story well told it is a story that stretches the boundaries of the human heart.

**"I am the only one who can tell
the story of my life and say what it means."**

—Dorothy Allison

Chapter 5

Traditional Tales

Listen to ...

1. **"Irish Tales of Death"**

   Guest Storyteller: Maxine Lennon, November 23, 2012

   Listen to the innovative way this brilliant teller weaves cultural ideology with fantasy and folklore. Here's to the Irish.

2. **"Spooky Tales"**

   Guest Storyteller: Brian Herod, October 31, 2013

   Listen to this perfect teller for the perfect scary tales given on the perfect autumn day. Be ready to hide under your blanket.

... and Watch

Sample student videos with commentary

Understand

Traditional story types
Parable
Selecting a story
Bedtime stories

*"Stories can conquer fear, you know.
They can make the heart bigger."*

—Ben Okri

Who and What Are They?

Although it is not the purpose of this text to discuss each of the story genres and their literary and performance implications for the teller, it is important to know that stories that originate from other people, cultures, and traditions are the ones from which many tellers model their personal narratives. Likewise, versatile storytellers should be equipped to tell a variety of stories from a number of categories. Therefore, a quick overview of story types can help you to both appreciate and understand what those categories can teach you about the art of telling.

A myth is a type of story designed to explain the inexplicable: clash between gods, climate change, changes in the configuration of the stars, falling in love, falling out of love, fielding restless children, and an abundance of scenarios that in our contemporary world are somewhat explained and more understood. For the bearer of the myth, the events described are true. A myth is based on belief.

According to many sources, the fairy tale and fantasy are discussed together without any real distinction. However, fairy tales seem to have their roots in archaic thought, and thus (in terms of historical time) immediately succeed the myth. Moreover, there are noteworthy differences between these two very similar genres. Traditional tellers of fairy tales try to preserve the story as close to its original version as possible. The protagonist's task in a fairy tale is impossible for an ordinary human to perform, and the tasks accomplished by the hero or heroine are symbolic or allegorical depictions. The time the tale takes place is also significant.

Originating from J. R. R. Tolkien's 1938 essay on *Fairy Stories*, fairy tales take place in one magical world, detached from our own world in both space and time. The traditional fairy tale sets the initial scene with its signature, "Once upon a time, (followed by the setting) . . . in a kingdom east of the moon . . ." Sometimes the scene is more concrete, but still more mythical than realistic. The time zone when a fairy tale takes place is in mythical time, the time when the story is well beyond reach for the listeners. The eternity of fairy tale time, expressed in the formula, "Lived happily ever after," enables the listener to remain in the fairy tale setting until the teller takes the listener back to the present state from which the story first began. Listeners are situated firmly outside of the story text.

A fantasy is a more conscious story creation, in that it tends to possess clearer story purposes (e.g., religious, philosophical, social, and satirical) than fairy tales. The fantastic experiences had by the protagonist in a fantasy are often dismissed as hallucinations, dreams, visions, or other types of delusional images caused, perhaps, by the character's emotional or psychological distress. These experiences are likely to have been produced by magic, a key factor in the fantasy.

Characters in a fantasy are often transported from a realistic setting (e.g., *Alice in Wonderland*, *The Wizard of Oz*) to some magical realm (*magical beings or objects, magical transformations*), and brought back safely to the present, or realistic setting. A fantasy, then, typically combines two worlds: our own real world and some other magical one.

Just as the fairy tale and fantasy are similar, so is the case when comparing the folktale to fable. In fact, the differences between these two genres are even more indiscernible than the aforementioned pair. Because folktales and fables are such popular choices for telling, we will explore them a bit more.

Most scholars agree that folktales (synonymous with folklore) are stories that begin with an oral telling about a significant tradition, custom, or quirky person from whom a lesson can be taken. Sometimes these stories take the form of song and nursery rhymes. Whatever their forms, these stories (which originate and belong to the "folk") are passed on through generations, and the lessons within them remain intact. These stories not only teach a lesson, but much like its literary cousin, the myth, a folktale oftentimes explains why things are as they are. Consider the abundance of superstitions that spring from folktales, especially those tales that derive from ancient religions or the supernatural (e.g., stories about apparitions) and charms (e.g., throwing salt over the shoulder or avoiding stepping on cracks on the pavement).

Folktales perpetuate the mystery of the number thirteen, as numerologists point to the notion that if you have thirteen letters in your name, you will have the devil's luck (e.g., Jack the Ripper, Charles Manson, Theodore Bundy, and Albert De Salvo). Stop worrying. If your name is comprised of thirteen letters, it does not mean you are doomed to a life as a serial killer. Remember, we are talking folktales.

Black cats, stepping under a ladder, even the humble mirror have roots from superstitious tales. In some cultures, mirrors in the home of a recently deceased family member must be covered to keep anyone from being tempted to look into the mirror, and thus losing his soul. In many Italian-American homes, placing the foot of the bed so that it faces the door points to the way the one who sleeps in that bed will be carried out in the case of his death. Talk about a tough time getting to sleep!

Folktales help to explain special days. Pumpkin (Jack-O-Lantern) carving originated in Eastern Europe. Before the pumpkin became the target of carving on Halloween, faces were carved from a turnip or rutabaga. The symbolic head was the most powerful part of the body, containing spirit and knowledge. Valentine's Day is one of the best illustrations of folktale in action. Characteristic of folktales, there are several versions of this special day of romance and love (and for using your credit card☺), each taking us down the same "tunnel of love," so to speak. Let's look at the Protestant and Catholic version.

Around 270 AD, a kindly priest, Saint Valentine, held secret marriage ceremonies for soldiers in opposition to King Claudius, who had prohibited marriage for young men (believing they would want to remain home with their wives rather than fight). No kidding, King! Though the ban on marriage was a great shock for Romans, they dared not voice their protest against the mighty emperor. For disobeying the order, Saint Valentine was executed on February 14, and in his dying breath said, "Love Conquers All!" OK, I made up the love conquers all thing. But did it change the integrity of the story? Remember, there are several versions, any of which take us down the path of one essential lesson: Love is everything. Acknowledge it. Celebrate it. And for goodness sakes don't forget it! And if you are interested enough to read other versions of Valentine's Day, or Halloween, St. Patrick's Day, and stories about Santa Claus (you do know he's folklore, right?), then you understand how folktales keep great traditions and customs alive.

One of the most important and intriguing things about a folktale is that the cultural history from which it is born often reflects the way the conflict (embedded in all stories, remember?) is solved in its mother culture. Also, an author of a folktale can impose a "partial muteness," in that he entertains us by providing a variety of cross-cultural and international stories that foretell lessons to be learned in both his, and our lives, rather than disclosing intimate and sentimental personal experiences which may have originally triggered those stories. One of my favorite examples of the innate conflict in a folktale and a lesson that may oblige us to forecast experiences in our lives is "The Strawberry." Story Origin: Zen Buddhist, Japan.

A Zen master had traveled to a distant village. As he was running late for his return train, he decided to take what he thought was a shortcut. He found himself walking along a steep path, staring off into the distance. So taken was he by the beauty of the view that he did not notice where he was walking. At that instant, he kicked a small stone and, a moment later, realized that he did not hear it land. He stopped, only to discover that he stood atop a huge cliff. Another step and he would have walked right off, to a hundred-foot drop below. As he stood there, gazing out at the mountains in the distance, he was suddenly shaken by a loud roar.

He turned around to see a huge tiger slowly approaching. He took a step to the side, only to have the ground crumble beneath his feet. Falling off the edge of the cliff, heels overhead, his hands reached out to grab whatever might save him. An instant later, he found himself clinging with one hand to a thorny vine, growing out of a crack in the rock. He looked up to the top of the cliff, where he saw the tiger, licking his lips. His eyes searched far below him, to the bottom of the cliff. There, looking up at him waited a second tiger. With one tiger above and another below, he looked again at the vine, its sharp thorns cutting into his hand. Near the vine, he saw a tiny mouse crawl out. It scampered along a tiny ledge to the vine, looked at him for a moment, then looked at the tiger, and finally began to gnaw at the vine.

The monk searched for anything else he might grab, but there was nothing. Then, far off to his side, he spotted a tiny plant. Surely, it was too small to hold his weight, but he reached for it just the same. It had green leaves, and as he parted them, he glimpsed something small and red. It was a wild strawberry plant, with one perfectly ripe strawberry. He plucked it from the plant and ate it. And as he did so he thought, "Isn't life sweet?"

Eating a strawberry? What a fool. He should be looking for a way to save his life. Did any of these thoughts pop into your head? However, this folktale teaches us about Buddhist ideology, with its premise securely anchored in the present and the appreciation of the moment. From the story's account, the chance of escape for the young Monk is impossible. If this story were born from another culture, the conflict and ultimate solution may be viewed from an entirely different perspective. But here is a question very much worth pondering: Would another ideology create a story with a character having no way out? I don't know. Nevertheless, folktales can teach their listeners to scrutinize complex circumstances in which they may find themselves. Buddhist thought advocates precious contemplation about life. This folktale does just that.

Because folktales are passed down through time and, as a result, become convoluted, the original authors are not likely to be known. Even the land of origin is sometimes in question. Therefore, the tellers own the stories they tell. They change the words, plots, even characters in many folktales and still manage to convey the story's fundamental lesson. Certainly, this does not mean that everyone in an audience who listens to the same folktale must agree to the lesson taught, but the storyteller should know the tale well enough so that whatever tampering he does will not totally distort the basic point of the story.

To illustrate, have four to six students in the same class read "The Strawberry" a few times, so that each can become comfortable with it. Keep the story a secret from the remainder of the class, who will serve as the listening audience. Have all but one of those (four to six) students leave the room. The lone student tells the story to the listeners (class). Then, with the same audience remaining in the room, another student enters, tells the story in his own words. The exercise continues long enough so that at least six students can tell the story their way. Discuss your observations. Were the versions similar? How did each teller own the story?

Another exercise designed to discover ways that the folktale can evolve and still maintain its common features is to try this: Pair up with a classmate. Select one of the two endings you see below. Working together, spend ten minutes creating a story and use your selected ending as the last lines to your tale. Design a story that will take no longer than three minutes to tell. Keep in mind that your story must end with the ending you choose.

"I think we have learned much today," he said. They embraced, and they danced for a long time between the darkness and the light.

Or

And on the rock, hidden beneath the old woman's rose bush, a tiny elf sat happily watching the party, one leg crossed over the other.

What did you think? Were there any similar story components conveyed by those pairs who selected the same ending? What do you remember from those stories with common endings? What were the common denominators used by the pairs charged with reaching the same story conclusion?

You do not need to examine the hundreds, perhaps thousands, of folktales found in print to discover how they evolve over time.

Think about how a folktale can emerge from your own life. Have you ever heard a story about a relative whom you never met? Did you ever notice how the story changes over time? My friend tells a wonderful story about his uncle. It goes like this:

"My Uncle Joe lived next door to my parents in an old apartment building in Brooklyn. My mother told me the story about how cheap my Uncle Joe was. He would come over to my parents' apartment every time my mother cooked in order to mooch a meal. Eventually, my mother got so tired of this; she would take a towel and place it under the door, to cover the crack, so that he wouldn't smell the fragrance from her cooking. Over the years, the story changed to her cooking on an unpredictable schedule to keep Uncle Joe away; to Uncle Joe going out to the fire escape to peek inside the window to determine when my mother was cooking . . . "

Arguably, this story can be categorized as a personal narrative. And it is indeed encased in personal narrative form. However, the heart of this story goes beyond personal reflection or direct observation, because the teller never met Uncle Joe. Uncle Joe was sort of a hero. Those who told it willingly and humorously over the years kept his eccentric personality alive. Sometimes a folktale can consist of a family member we know very well. Remember the story about Valentine's Day? Well, not all such folktales are for the romantic. My colleague, Jere Phister, tells this story told to her by her mother, one that combines superstition with a family member she knew very well:

"She always said the reason she and my father were divorced was that she wore a green suit at their wedding. Green was a bad color for the bride to wear. It didn't matter that my father was a drunk and always mean. I think that's why she wore green, to ensure that she could get out of the marriage. She could just blame her bad judgment on the color of her dress."

As with Jere's mother, I guess it is fair to say that a folktale can give its originator a reason for why something went wrong. These stories become folklore or where I come from, "bubbe maisse" (Yiddish for grandmother's tale). They are not unlike the folktales in print (see sources listed at the end of the next section on "choosing a story to tell"), which consist of those whimsical, unique, and beloved characters who live on forever in our hearts and minds to keep traditions, customs, and lessons about the human spirit very much alive.

I don't want to muddy the water that has already produced a somewhat cloudy definition of folktale. Still, I will induce a small mudslide in order to introduce a few offshoots: the tall tale, legend, and urban legend. A kind of folktale, the tall tale is an extravagant, fanciful, or greatly exaggerated story. Tall tales usually focus on the achievement of a hero with superhuman strength and skill (e.g., Pecos Bill, Paul Bunyan). Legends are traditional tales based on a few specks of historical accuracy (e.g., Jesse James, Davey Crockett). Urban legends (synonymous with urban myths) are as apocryphal stories, involving fantastic circumstances, yet laced with a tantalizing bit of plausibility to them. Propelled by small grains of truth, the urban legend also commonly uses elements of fear, horror, and mystery to convey cautionary tales (e.g., *Vanishing Hitchhiker, Alligators in the Manhattan Sewers*).

Urban legends are sometimes created by adults to frighten children. What makes these tales especially frightening is that they contain that crumb of truth. Urban legends usually contain some evolving character, making the chap in the story applicable to many cultures. After all, lots of parents, regardless from where they come, can resort to silly manipulation techniques. To illustrate the evolving character of the urban legend, let's look at the Boogeyman.

The Boogeyman is the living embodiment of all that children fear. It is a word used to convey the generic scary person who lurks under a child's bed or peeks through the crack of the closet. Although many versions abound, it is the Czech version that is most frightening. There once was some dastardly creature that resembled a man who hid in riverbanks, making sounds like a lost baby to lure adults as well as children. I know, it makes me shiver too. But remember this is an evolving character. So, in Scotland, the Boggart was a malicious fairy who causes personal calamities. Not to worry, because most Scots will tell you a horseshoe over the doorway leading to the fairy's hideaway will protect you from him.

In England the baggy-man drove a cart to pick up corpses during the Black Plague that decimated Europe. That's correct, there really was a Black Plague, there were a number of documented calamities in Scotland, and there was a very bad person who lured and hurt several people in Czechoslovakia over a century and a half ago. Now, can you say urban legend? There are Dutch, Japanese, and French versions of this terrible fellow, each custom-designed to create the right fear factor for its home culture. The Boogeyman has indeed evolved and exists today in the minds of parents who love to scare. Shame on them.

Additional snooping into folklore points to the fable as a kind of folktale. However, with a bit of probing, it becomes clear that a fable is a short narrative with three defining features: brevity; the use of animals to personify human characteristics; and it contains a moral, such as the value of cooperation or looking at a problem from different points of view.

Although some fables contain human characters, the animals rule: "The Bat and the Weasels," "The Cat and the Mice," "The Cat and the Birds," "The Tortoise and the Hare," "The Bee and Jupiter" (inanimate object, not a human), and "The Quack Frog," to name a few of my favorites, represent the quick-witted fable. Animals are symbolic and culturally adorned in a fable. In fact, different cultures tend to use different animal tricksters in fables from their lands. North American fables use coyotes, hares, and ravens. African fables employ the tortoise, Anasi the Spider, and Zomo the Hare. Japan uses the badger. Europe introduces the fox and wolf as tricksters.

Even though the conflict is readily apparent in a fable, the moral is typically not stated as directly as it might in a folktale. Aesop's "The Bear and the Fox" illustrates this well:

A bear was once bragging about his generous feelings, and saying how refined he was compared with other animals. (There is, in fact, a tradition that a bear will never touch a dead body). A fox, who heard him talking in this strain, smiled and said, "My friend, when you are hungry, I only wish you would confine your attention to the dead and leave the living alone."

The meaning of the Bear and Fox is uncertain at best. Some fables have multiple layers of meaning (Indian tales, for instance). Other types of fables with indirect lessons include "Why" or "Porquoi" stories. Short of an assigned parable, which is a designated use of language purposively intended to convey a hidden meaning other than that contained in the words themselves ("Slow and steady wins the race"), the fable tests the interpretive ability of its listeners as they pour over the founding moral in a formidable maze of magic and more.

The variety of traditional stories is nothing less than a comprehensive treasure chest of wonder. Heavily soaked in cultural roots, folktales, including tall tales and legends, are simple and straightforward stories that teach us lessons in wisdom, courage, confidence, and good against evil. The narrative power we find in fables is astounding as they render us morally responsible for our actions. Explanations once found in great myths have led us to advanced thinking about ways to field those complex and staggering events that give us reasons for pause. Fairy tales are filled with the magic we sometimes need to fuel our dreams. We see worlds shift in a fantasy and return to the present time we suddenly see as precious. We love their stories. We always will.

Which Stories to Tell?

If you have ever gone searching for the perfect puppy, you will know that sometimes the best way to find the right one is to let the puppy pick you. Hannah, my mini dachshund (actually with her eating habits she's inching toward full size) was one of five females in the litter (as in the film, *Hannah and Her Sisters* ☺). When she and the other cuties were placed on the floor, I got down there with them, and Hannah was the kisser of the group. Her unflinching affection certainly won me over. She's been kissing ever since.

Picking a story can work in a similar way. Go to the children's section of your favorite bookstore or library, pull some books off the shelves, get down on the floor, skim them over, and find out which one speaks to you. If this method does not suit you, then here are some more conventional ways to make your selection.

Selecting the type of story you want to tell is not much different from the way you choose your narrative, that being by reflecting on significant memories. Do you have favorite stories from your childhood? Are there any stories that made you feel good, safe, or special? Asking these questions can be a terrific start when deciding on a folktale, fable, fairy tale, or any type of "their" stories, including personal narratives delivered by friends and relatives whom you cherish, and whose stories you wish to retain and retell.

Choose to tell a story you like, and be sure it is a story relevant and appropriate to your target audience. What lesson or moral do you want to peddle to your listeners? Scouring libraries and bookstores that categorize stories in themes, (e.g., hope, bullies, compassion, telling the truth, respect, love, care, loss, disappointment, fairness, and so on) can help you filter through some wonderful story possibilities. You will also want to consider the setting in which you will tell the story. Will you be telling a story to children in a classroom? Are you planning to tell a story to an audience of different cultures, ethnicities, and ages at a cultural arts festival?

If you plan to tell a story in a bookstore, auditorium, or even at a birthday party, there is call for other important considerations. When telling a story as part of a children's creative drama program or educational training, planning the placement of the story can determine how the message will be heard. As long as we are on the subject of story selections for children, let us consider some additional ways to select for the young'uns out there so we can have an even better chance at piquing their interest and getting them to love storytelling.

Try to find a story that includes rhythm and word repetition, especially if your audience is comprised of kids seven years and younger. Rhythm and repetition (e.g., "I do like green eggs and ham, I do, I do, Sam I am") represent play, and play is motivating for children (as well as for adults). If your story selection contains animals, have fun with animal voices, and let the kids help you create animal sounds.

If you are selecting children's folktales, consider stories with characters having brothers and sisters and close friends so that your young audience can better relate to the relationships that cultivate between significant characters in the story, as well as the conflict those characters will encounter. Children aged ten to early teens tend to enjoy stories of real-life heroes as well as science fiction (*Harry Potter*). Conversely, stories that appeal to children of all ages are stories that also teach them about a world worth discovering.

Choices of stories are indeed infinite, but I hope these basic suggestions help you to feel more confident about the selections you make. Whatever choice you make for whatever type of audience, know that you are doing something very special when you tell them a story. In some way, you help them travel down a long, imaginative road very far away to find out what may be closest to their hearts.

Sweet Dreams

Let's talk bedtime stories. They are essential to any well-adjusted child. Reading stories to children at bedtime is one of the best ways to stimulate their imagination. Stories best suited for bedtime typically utilize the techniques of visualization to help the child enter the story by relaxing his mind and imagining himself a part of a beautiful setting. Creating a picture in his mind is an important way in which a child can develop the power of imagination, and can give him a sense of control over his thinking. By helping a child build his own picture of the action in the story, you teach him how to detach from daily concerns and explore new possibilities. Indeed, this creative exploration can be useful for solving problems and in setting priorities.

Although there are no hard, fast rules to telling stories at bedtime, a teller should keep his voice calm but still expressive and enthusiastic. A story at bedtime should be enjoyable and peaceful. If reading the story is a teller's preference, then illustrations contained in the story can serve as a launching pad for creative ideas. Therefore, pictures should be displayed at an appropriate and meaningful pace. Moreover, illustrations, whether they are shown to a child during the story or conveyed through gestures, postures, and the like can enhance his understanding of the story significantly. Consider how a child would find it difficult to comprehend words like refuel, re-assess, and momentum, but would become fully engaged by the illustration—shown, said, or both "Rolling backwards before building up enough strength to move up the hill" in *The Little Engine That Could*.

Even after this discussion I can only surmise about the proper features of a bedtime story. Still, here are some additional recommendations I can comfortably add to those mentioned above:

It should be short;

It shouldn't give kid nightmares;

The story should invite repetition (kids love hearing it over and over);

It should come from a specific genre (short versions of fairytale, myth, fable, etc.);

It should be fun;

It should be very well known to the teller (telling, not reading it); and

We should want to hear it again, but can't… *It's time for Nighty Night.*

Now, get some sleep.

Get to the Source

Here are some of my favorite sources for myths, fantasies, fairy tales, fables, and folktales: *Complete Fairy Tales of the Brothers Grimm*, edited by Jack Zipes; *Arrow to the Sun: A Pueblo Indian Tale*, by Gerald McDermott; *The Children of Odien: Nordic Gods and Heroes*, by Padraic Colum and Thomas DuBois; *Fifty Famous Fairy Tales,* by Rosemary Kingston; *The Wisdom of Fairy Tales*, by Rudolf Meyer; *American Indian Fairy Tales*, by Margaret Compton; *Little Book of Fairy Tales*, by Veronica Uribe and Gisela Arevado; *European Folk and Fairy Tales*, by Joseph Jacobs; *Tales Our Abuelitas Told: A Hispanic Folklore Collection*, by Ada Campey; *Young Warriors: Stories of Strength,* by Pierce and Sherman; *Around the World in 80 Tales*, by Priotta and Johnson; *Myths, Legends, and Folktales of America,* by Leeming, Page and Page; *Best Loved Folktales from Around the World*, compiled by Joanna Cole; *Multicultural Folktales: Stories to Tell Young Children*, by Judy Sierra and Robert Kaminski; *The Family Storytelling Book*, by Jack Maguire; *Joining in: An Anthology of Audience Participation Stories and How to Tell Them*, by a collection of practicing storytellers; and *Twenty Tellable Tales*, by Margaret MacDonald; *Enchantment of the Faerie Realm*, by Ted Andrews; *Fairy Magic*, by Rosemary Ellen Guiley; *The Element Encyclopedia of Magical Creatures*, by John Matthews and Caitlin Matthews; *An Anthology of Finnish Folktales*, by Helena Henderson; *Favorite African Folktales*, by Nelson Mandela; *Retold Mexican American Folktales*, by Esther Cervantes; *Retold Northern European Myths*, by PLC Editors; and *The People Could Fly: An American Black Folktales*, by Virginia Hamilton, Leo Dillon, and Diane Dillon.

There are also hundreds of resourceful sites available to you. Here are three very good ones:

www.storyarts.org

www.aaronshep.com/storytelling/bookshelf

Search the stacks, sites, and story groups (see references and resources) for countless ideas and guidance. Remember your copyright responsibilities if you tell a story outside of a library or classroom setting. Always give credit to the author, and if the author is unknown, it is good form to say so.

Final Remarks...

Traditional stories carry a special power for engaging the imagination. From fairy tales to myths to folklore and more, these tales born of culture and traditions speak to us about unsettled times, a hopeful future, and profoundly felt truths. Although these yarns do not document our lives, they are united with our fondest memories and will forever continue to reach deeply into our hearts. These stories make magic appear before our eyes.

"Fairy tales are more than true: not because they tell us that dragons exist, but because they tell us that dragons can be beaten."

—G. K. Chesterton

Chapter 6

Parts of a Story

© Everett Collection/Shutterstock.com

Listen to ...

1. **"All Features Included"**

   Guest Storyteller: Rabbi Laura Sheinkopft,
   March 13, 2014

   Listen to how this teller takes all the required features of a story and uses them to deliver a remarkably fluid, coherent, and funny set of religious yarns. You will be praying for more.

2. **"Back to School"**

   Guest Storyteller: Jere Pfister and Scott Bumgardner,
   August 8, 2008

   Listen how these hilarious tellers revive their long lost school days by retrieving all the tension they felt from teachers, tests, and bullies . . . followed by a barrage of quick-hitters on school supplies.

Understand

Parts of a story
Dialectical tension
SAC
Prologue
Epilogue
Intrigue
Tone
Theme
Motif

*"Who makes you storyteller? You do. You are.
Go play."*

—Will Hindmarch

Common Aspects

Whatever the ages of the target listeners or the type of story delivered, a story is only real if it resonates with them. Stories that fail to pack the necessary punch unleash nothing more than meaningless words, murky themes, confusing characters, and a waste of time for the audience. If, on the other hand, a story is carefully crafted for the audience, their expectations (often unconscious) of the experience can be completely met. The vigilance with which a teller molds a story depends on how well that storyteller understands the parts of a story, as well as his capacity for skillfully using them. Let me give you a ridiculously short course on those parts that bind a story of any kind and how those fixed components can help you tell a tale. The necessary parts to a story include a starting point, character, setting, plot, tension/conflict (causing a problem), and an ending.

"Once upon a time," is the traditional starting point in a children's story. In a personal narrative, prefacing remarks (prologue) are needed to set the scene, possibly introduce the characters, establish the tone, and create a sense of inquiry and interest for the audience. Types of characters can range from those who are familiar, realistic, and common (e.g., your neighbor, friends at school, family, and teachers) to characters who are familiar, semi-realistic, and uncommon (e.g., folk heroes, giants, kings, queens, witches).

Characters can also be imaginary or "stylized" (e.g., dragons, aliens from outer space, monsters). Whatever the story type, the main character or hero is the protagonist, while the worthy adversary (if one is present) is the antagonist. Development in story characters can have a range of dimensions from polarized "flat" characters found primarily in children's stories (e.g., poor/rich; little/big; beautiful/ugly; nice/wicked; young/old; wise/stupid) to those characters with complex and shifting emotions found in adult prose.

Where the story takes place is the setting (e.g., a kingdom, picnic grounds, amusement park, Neverland). Whether the story is true or a tall tale with an impossible or implausible scheme, the plot must be developed. When the plot "thickens," it is because there is tension between characters or a series of obstacles that a character must overcome. This tension is where we identify the problem, and the conflict appears when we witness the struggles of the protagonist and the way he solves his dilemma. The protagonist makes difficult choices, and we hope, for the hero's sake, that they work. Clearly defined moral choices and actions (characteristic in fables) are a common decision made by most characters. This kind of decision can provide the ultimate point of reflection for an audience.

The punch line, morally significant line, rhythmic or lyrical line, poignantly dramatic, and formulated ("they lived happily ever after") are types of lines designed to signify a story's closure. Sometimes, a closing remark, or epilogue (the only aspect of a story that is optional) can more clearly state the moral or practical deduction of a story. The teller delivers this closing remark after the story is completed. A deliberate pause combined with looking down can effectively cue an audience that a short epilogue is forthcoming.

From Start

Over the years, I have found that students experience a bit more angst about creating effective prologues and optional epilogues for their stories than almost anything else. Well, I aim to please. Here is a more comprehensive discussion of how to begin and end your story.

In her book, *Storytelling and the Art of Imagination*, Nancy Mellon concedes that beginnings are like births, because "They have emptiness and openness. They offer a place of warm receptivity into which the listener can safely arrive." She views the beginning of a story as a time not when the first words of the story are recited, but when the storyteller's internal thoughts help him to build enough momentum to become immediate (accessible) to his audience.

I know many novice storytellers who think it is easier to tell a children's story because it provides the standard, "Once upon a time" (OUAT). This novice impression would make great sense to Nancy Mellon: "*Once* brings a sense of immediacy; *upon* lifts the storyscape up into imagination; *a time* takes you and your listeners both forward and backward, until you arrive at a point of creative stillness from which the happenings of the story can creatively unfold." Since most of the stories we tell are personal narratives and do not begin with the formulated OUAT (although I suppose they could), new storytellers often don't know how or where to begin.

The easiest way to choose a beginning to a story is to ask yourself one fundamental question: "Why does this story matter to me?" When you answer this question, you add more to your prologue than sketchy information about the scene, tone, and characters. You are now able to communicate to your listeners that the story you are about to tell is planned for them. This storyteller to audience connection (SAC) is a requirement for every successful teller, and the better the SAC, the stronger the relationship between the teller and listeners. Look at the opening to this hypothetical narrative without a prologue.

The figure would reach out as if to grab my leg and I would wake at precisely the moment before he would reach the foot of my bed. Each night I would wake at precisely 11:55 and my father, with equal precision, would come to my room at 11:57 only to hear me scream with utter fear, the kind of scream you might hear manufactured in a haunted house . . .

Consider the same narrative segment preceded by this prologue:

All of us have had nightmares. When we are awakened by them, our sweat and cries quickly turn to deep breaths and a sense of calm, thanks to our parents' loving embrace. Nightmares are, after all, the stuff of dreams. For me, one repeated nightmare was born of truth or at least truth as I knew it. "The figure would reach . . . "

Creative placement of the prologue can evoke different responses from an audience. The example above shows the prologue positioned commonly at the outset of the story. Sometimes, a teller can intensify the drama by beginning the story, then stopping after a few moments to deliver the prologue. Then continue with the story.

Begin story: *He handed me money with the kind of generosity of heart I never thought would be possible for him. I saw him in a different light. Different light? Hell, it was the first time I thought he even cared . . .*

Prologue: *Remember times when you'd ask your Mom, "Is Dad in a good mood?" If he were, you would ask him for money. If not, well, you'd wait. He was in a bad mood all right but I decided not to wait. I'm glad I didn't. I met my father for what seemed to be the first time that night.*

Continue story: *Don't misunderstand me. I knew he cared. He just didn't know how to show it. But when he put his hand in his pocket and took out a wad of bills, I wasn't sure if he was . . .*

Dialogue can also be an effective ingredient in a prologue:

"What did you say?" I asked. My friend, somewhat shy, tepidly answered, "I said I have been chosen as a representative on the U.S. Gymnastics team at the Olympics," she repeated. Hey, don't get me wrong. I was happy for her. But . . . (tell story).

I want to return to OUAT for a moment. Contrary to very popular belief, "Once upon a Time" is often not strong enough a starting point. Since these stories have been published, it is essential to include the author (unless unknown) and title in the prologue. Here are some examples:

It's important to take care of our things. If we don't we might learn a very hard lesson, just as the Princess learned in the "Frog Prince," *by Jacob and Wilhelm Grimm.*

Sometimes it's easy to give up. Things are hard and we don't think we can do it. But most of the time we can. We just have to try to realize that the only way to fail is not to try. The Little Engine learned it. Let's find out how in "The Little Engine That Could" by Watty Piper.

Adapting to an audience happens through the thoughtful way in which a teller can creatively connect a story's theme with the audience who needs to hear it. For example, even the same children's story can be meaningful to a variety of audiences if the teller configures his prologue appropriately. Consider the following adaptations for telling Dr. Seuss' "The Sneetches," to three different audiences:

To Kids: *We all know it isn't good to pick on others. All of us are important and special and are terrific the way we are. We need to accept each other and not change just to fit in. If you don't believe me, just listen to what happens to* "The Sneetches," *by Dr. Seuss.*

To Parents: *I know that it's difficult to explain the destructive forces of narrow-mindedness and prejudice to our children. But it might be time to let someone else do the explaining for us.* "The Sneetches," *by Dr. Seuss, has helped children ponder the nature of prejudice in a way they can understand. Before you read this special story to your children, listen to it yourself.* "The Sneetches," *by Dr. Seuss.*

To Student Teachers: *Being charged with teaching tolerance to first graders is daunting, to say the least.* "The Sneetches," *by Dr. Seuss, might help you to convey the framework from which solid discussion about stereotyping can come, and a story with the powerful interactive component needed to make the wonderful characters in the story come to life.*

Storytellers help an audience move from an everyday world into the world of story. One way to do this is to treat the act of coming together to share a story as something special. Like a birthday, anniversary, holiday, or any special day or rite of passage, the storytelling gives the event a sense of occasion. This sense of the occasion is best contrived and told in the teller's prologue, where the overall purpose and tone of the story are clearly conveyed. Special days are portrayed in the prologue a number of different ways. Here are some illustrations:

We all love birthdays, especially when it's ours. And today is mine! Hurrah! We love the presents, good wishes, ice cream, cake, and all the fun that comes with a day that belongs to us. But what would happen if you thought everyone forgot your birthday? I mean everyone: your mom and dad, your friends, your teacher. Everyone. That sounds pretty sad, doesn't it? Well, I was convinced everyone forgot mine when . . .

Today marks the first day of Hanukkah, the festival of lights. Benny couldn't wait for tonight, because not only would he get his Hanukkah present, but his Mom was making his favorite Hanukkah meal, potato pancakes and applesauce. Not only that, but Benny's Uncle Sol was coming over for dinner and he knew that Uncle Sol could tell the story of Hanukkah better than anyone in the world, in "Uncle Sol's Potato Pancake Party," by Cynthia Levine.

My cousin Charlie always had the greatest smile, told the funniest jokes, and never forgot to say good morning to anyone who crossed his path. I think about him today, Memorial Day. But the truth is I think about him every day. The moment Aunt Betty called me to tell me that Charlie was killed in Iraq was the moment I started to think about him every day. I remember thinking that Charlie loved Spiderman, because he thought he was the coolest of the super heroes. Charlie was the greatest super hero of them all. I remember the time when he . . .

Halloween is just around the corner, right? And on Halloween, very peculiar and scary things can happen. These scary things can even happen to "The Little Old Lady Who Wasn't Afraid of Anything," by Jeanne O'Dair.

As family and friends, you all know my parents. Yet on their thirty-fifth wedding anniversary, I thought it might be fun to share a story that will heighten the love we all have for them already. It was 1997, late Thursday afternoon, when Fritz, a German Shepherd puppy, sheepishly strolled up the front walk of my parents' home . . .

It's February 14th and I can only think of the most beautiful girl I ever saw. She's all I can think about on Valentine's Day. She is, and remains the love of my life. I knew it the moment I opened the door . . .

Intrigue, another potentially powerful slice in the prologue pie, can intensify the teller's connection with his audience. Intrigue is the arousal of curiosity and in storytelling is portrayed through mystery and suspense. Mystery can render listeners baffled and perplexed, while suspense can trigger a sense of anxious anticipation in the audience. Both keep listeners on edge and keep them "intrigued" as they await the unpredictable. Consider these examples:

Mystery: *The candy bar just sat there on the counter, partly opened, as if Ken was coming back for it. But here's the thing: That brand of candy bar hasn't been manufactured since 1986, the year Ken died.*

Suspense: *"You know that saying about living every day as if it's your last? It's true, except for the day you die." Kevin Spacey, from the movie* American Beauty.

Listeners can feel another kind of intrigue when a teller describes part of the story as being in "close range," or distance to them. A teller's use of range might be:

Close Range: *You better not think that, because he's right around the corner, or closer; maybe even . . . under your bed.*

To Finish

The great majority of published wise old tales end happily. These natural story endings parallel the OUAT beginnings. However, unlike a carefully crafted prologue, the epilogue is an optional part of a story. It is used when the story does not speak for itself or when the plot is too intricate or the characters too confounding to deconstruct in the limited amount of time you have to tell the tale. In addition, an epilogue can punctuate a point, pose a question for reflection, or foster discussion. Teachers who use storytelling as an instructional method frequently use a well-framed epilogue to clarify the learning objectives their students were to acquire from the story. After telling the story of "Phaethon, Son of Apollo," by

Olivia Coolidge, to a group of fourth graders in a story dramatization workshop, I delivered the following epilogue:

Sometimes we ask our moms and dads to do things that we know are wrong, figuring if they really love us they will do them for us anyway. Phaethon talked his dad into doing the wrong thing and his dad was a god. You don't get much smarter than that. But Apollo still did the wrong thing. It is important not to take advantage of someone we love, thinking it will be a way of getting what we want. That is very wrong, and love is way too important.

I improvised the epilogue. I could tell at the end of the story that the kids needed a little more closure than what the story itself could provide. The epilogue, then, can be a valuable way to cipher through a story's unforeseen muckiness, and give the storyteller a chance to recover and revise the story's message for his listeners. Perhaps the most common and effective way to use an epilogue is to share a personal reflection, revelation, or comment with your listeners. To deliver an epilogue, it is best to look at the ground and pause (*for about three seconds*) after you have completed the story. Then, raise your head, maintain eye contact, and deliver your epilogue:

I cannot fathom a story with greater meaning for me. It is a story enriched with soul.

Learning about selfishness hurt me and hit me harder than I ever realized. It will hit you too. Just wait!

Not buried is not entirely true, because she's really buried deep in my heart.

At this point, you should have a good understanding of the parts of a story. However, one of the more interesting and complex components of every story is conflict. Conflict is the heart of the drama in a story, and because I want to be sure that there is no conflict about understanding the essence of conflict, let us explore it a bit more.

Conflict

Sometimes I will ask adults in my storytelling workshops what they see as the conflict in "Little Red Riding Hood." These very bright, very animated parents and teachers respond with things like, "What kind of mother sends her daughter into the woods?" "If Grandmother was so sick, why did the mother leave her alone in a small house so very far away?" "I don't think any mother could be as stupid as to not plan in advance . . ."

These responses are not unexpected. Psychologist Eric Berne would agree with those interpretations, because he thought fairy tales defied logic and, as a result, caused internal conflict for anyone who tried to make sense out of them, including those passionate participants in my storytelling sessions. However, these interpretations, perhaps logical and well intended by discerning parents, dedicated behaviorists, and excessively analytical teachers are not really conflict at all. Rather it is a series of interpretations made by responsible adults whose idea of conflict is any questionable motive displayed by a story's relevant character, or a central character's moral conduct.

Those sound like legitimate concerns and certainly are catalysts for meaningful discussion. However, the impressions we have about the kind of mother who raised Little Red should not burden us. Conflict is an objective, deliberative component in a story, and it occurs when a central character has a goal and a series of obstacles that prevent the goal from being met. Sometimes conflict is a clash or dispute between or within characters. Therefore, we need to worry about Red Riding Hood finding her way out of a jam, and not whether to call Child Protective Services.

Because children's stories are models of conflict found in any type of story, continuing a discussion about story conflict by following the path of a children's fairy tale makes sense. Bruno Bettelheim presents the fairy tale as a story type designed to get across to the child that a struggle against severe difficulties in life is unavoidable, because it is an intrinsic part of human existence (Just ask

Alexander in *Alexander and the Terrible, Horrible, Very Bad Day* by Judith Viorst).

Bettelheim proposes that the fairy tale "expresses in words and actions the things which go on in children's minds." Hansel and Gretel must learn that their mother is their protective shield and source of nourishment and love to which they must return once they find their way out of darkness. The children must solve a problem. The re-building of the relationship (overcoming obstacles and stopping a dispute) between mother and children, as in the case of *Hansel and Gretel,* is a familiar conflict found in many children's stories. Softer, more subtle conflicts are found in folktales and fables (see *"Their"* stories), and an infinite variety of conflict scenarios serve as the core in our personal narratives.

The source for most of the conflict in our personal narratives is our interpersonal relationships. After all, isn't that where we clash with other characters? Isn't that the context in which we try to overcome a surplus of obstacles? How do we break up with him? How do I tell my parents that I'm not coming in for their fiftieth anniversary? How can I tell the doctor that I'm mad that he kept me waiting for almost two hours? Do the words, "We need to talk" ruin your day? No one greeted you at work? Then there are the attractive opposites. Conflict can produce tension and the greatest tension comes from a theme with two elements that don't ordinarily go together: helpless doctors, toothless dental hygienists, advisors who have no advice to offer, make the story. Tension can add humor or tragedy and ultimately becomes the tale's climactic moment as well as its central point.

Most interpersonal conflict is either external or internal. Both forms are prevalent in stories of all types. Understanding the nature of these conflict forms can assist a storyteller in addressing the drama in a story more vividly. Researchers have long known that external conflict occurs when two people have opposing or incompatible forces that exist simultaneously. For example, a husband comes home, excited to tell his wife about his promotion, which, among other things, will require that the couple move across the country.

He might be greeted with, "I'm not moving. I like it here. My parents are here, the kids love their school, and I hate moving." This example represents the tension caused by two opposing needs (one desiring change, the other desiring predictability). "I need a couple of evenings to myself" will be in opposition to a partner who thrives on the expectation that "I thought we would do everything together." This tension stretches the band of autonomy versus connection. There are many more examples of such opposition, the kind of opposition between story characters that prompts a listener to proclaim, "Ah, the plot thickens."

Research has also revealed that internal conflict tends to surface when a person is somehow constrained by his moral values, such as the husband who is considering cheating on his wife, but is held back by his moral consciousness. You know your best friend stole a camera from Target. Do you confront him? Thinking it's a one-dollar bill, you accidentally put a five-dollar bill in the hat of a blind man. Do you retrieve it? Ask for change? Do you leave it in his hat and walk away? Internal and external conflict is the stuff great stories are made of.

Whether it is a story about the most intense tragedy or one about the most trivial dilemma, there is some form of conflict found in every story of every kind. With every conflict, characters struggle not only with a defined problem, but traditionally must field that problem in a challenging setting (*How do I leave the ball? How do I get out of seeing my in-laws? Can I make it to school on time? Should I pick up the phone and speak to her? What alternative treatment is available for my dad? How do I get a job? Where is that Prince? How many frogs must I kiss? And so on . . .*). Okay, we have obstacles, disputes, nice characters and brutes, troubles and woes, and a rash of clash (a little poem for levity).

Solving conflict requires problem-solving, and problem-solving is an important benefit of storytelling. Because storytelling encourages creative thinking, it can teach us new perspectives on ways to solve problems. Let's experiment with storytelling the way children might use it to handle sticky situations. Below you will see pairs of strange, unrelated characters matched with a problem and a setting. Get together with a classmate, choose a pair/problem/setting option (better yet have your instructor assign them), and create a story dialogue using those given characters to somehow get out of the mess both of you share. Be sure to include the setting, because that will oftentimes serve as the backdrop. For example, a clever pig and giant child stuck in the attic. The clever pig and giant child are obviously the characters with "being stuck" as the problem, and the attic as the setting. There are many creative avenues you might take when forming this story. It is best to start with a synopsis:

The giant child gets stuck in the attic while playing, and the clever pig (who can speak) talks the child down from the attic, by issuing carefully articulated instructions, much like an air traffic controller talking to a pedestrian on how to land a plane without panic emerging from either party.

Then in dialogue form:

"Hey, are you up there? Your mother will be home in a bit and be angry with you."
"Is that you, pig?"
"Oh, so I'm only a pig, am I?"
"OK, Sylvester. Sorry."
"Not important now. We must find a way to get you down from there. I am too large to retrieve you."
"Well, I'm big."
"Yes, with a small brain."
"What did you say?"
"Nothing! Now, let's get started."

Take ten minutes to create your story (synopsis recommended) and use dialogue between the characters (improvise and have fun) to tell the story. Creatively incorporate the setting, and try to solve the problem. Got it? Go!

giant/midget
getting out of a snowstorm
on a mountain

anteater/fairy godmother
lost
in Antarctica

Jewish mother/basketball player
hungry
in a canoe

clown/accountant
need for money
at a circus

old man/undertaker
looking for work
at a donut shop

bartender/musician
confused
the *Titanic*

shy person/motivational speaker
scared
New York Times Square

slow leopard/fast turtle
running away
railroad crossing

make up your own
anything goes
anyplace works

What did you think? Weird? You are in a storytelling course, not
organic chemistry. How did you and your partner solve the
problem? How did you field the setting? How did you pursue your
dialogue? Along with viewing conflict as a natural and necessary
ingredient in any story, this exercise pushed you and your partner
into the brink of sudden brilliance by producing some astonishing
learning outcomes. For example, when you paired up with a

classmate to address the problem and setting, you could not solve the problem by criticizing the strange attributes of your partner. Instead, you had to listen and learn to access your partner's/character's resources. There was no time to argue, reject each other, or be despondent. You had to work together. You did not have the chance to say, "I don't want to be stuck with a slow leopard." You had no choice. You found the best that each of you/character had to offer and used those assets to solve the problem.

It was brilliant when you learned to respect, accept, and tolerate each other. Learning to resolve conflict isn't just a matter of identifying the cause; it's a matter of learning how to open your mind, develop innovative ideas, and collaborate with others with whom you may initially not have much in common. You found common ground. You behaved the way people should. All of us should interact with others the way you interacted with your partner. You demonstrated this, and that is truly astonishing.

Along with acquiring skills in creative decision-making and collaborative problem-solving, it is no wonder why researchers in elementary education have long advocated storytelling as a way to teach tolerance and active listening successfully. Can you think of any group who might benefit from learning to listen to others more actively, to become more tolerant of those who are different from themselves, and in developing their skills in creative decision-making and collaborative problem-solving? You are correct. The world.

Themes and Motifs

Themes and motifs are essential to any story. Often a motif and theme are seen as synonyms, but they do differ somewhat. The theme is the central idea in a story. It is the constant thread with which the story is anchored. Any number of narrative elements with symbolic significance can be classified as motifs. These may be images, spoken or written phrases, structured or stylistic devices, or other elements like sound, physical movement, or visual components in dramatic narratives. Themes can unfold naturally for listeners as the teller conveys a story, and can also emerge from the storyteller's openly disclosing the theme along with the meandering motifs that reinforce it. Typically, a theme is abstract, open to an assortment of interpretations made by a range of listeners. The motif is concrete.

For example, a motif to reinforce the element of the destruction of a family in a story could come from shattered glass, an unfaithful spouse, or a runaway teen. Oftentimes a motif can be a contrast, like, "light and dark." A candle, ominous clouds, a rainbow, or a tunnel might be how life resumes itself. In fables and folktales motifs can include talking animals, triumph of poor over rich, tricksters, castles, wishes, deep sleep or trances, or recurring patterns or numbers, just to name a few. Fairies are oftentimes a motif for community or cohesion. Many motifs found in fairy tales support wishes coming true, having enough food, and finding your children. Regardless of type of tale told, what is especially useful for a storyteller is that themes and motifs are not important because they work together to make a story more intelligible, rather they work together to add and sustain interest. Motifs keep us engaged and themes keep us on track. Examine the motifs in this excerpt taken from Billy Crystal's *700 Sunday's*.

"I saw the strangest thing today. The car wouldn't start. I'm on my way to my dad's funeral and the damn car won't start. I called Stan. He was going to the funeral anyways. And Stan, the service man from the local gas station, was trying to start it. He and Dad worked on the car for years together and they kept it running perfectly. Stan always had a smile. Now he was sad. He became sadder with every turn of the ignition key. It wouldn't turn over. Stan's face was determined. But hey the battery died . . . . I wish there was a way that you could edit people out of your life, like it was a movie. You cut out people who are happy or sad depending on what you want. The person I wanted to cut out was the funeral director at the funeral home, which ironically was in the shadows of Yankee Stadium in the Bronx. My life had just fallen apart."

What do you think is the theme? Is there more than one? What are the motifs that support your impressions? Crystal's unyielding, almost merciless twisting and blending of feelings with sudden observations reveal the consequence of well-placed motifs while whittling away in search for a promising theme.

Final Remarks...

Storytellers who can skillfully manipulate the parts of a story are able to combine a mesmeric character (could be you), captivating setting, and exhilarating tension with a powerful prologue and, if needed, memorable epilogue into a package they can proudly deliver to their listeners. Knowing the parts of a story is like knowing the anatomy of a story, complete with the knowledge about the essential systems that need to run smoothly in order to keep the story healthy and well.

"There once was a Norwegian farmer who loved his wife so much . . . he almost told her."

—Minnesota folk saying

Chapter 7

Painting the Spoken Picture

© Alexy Losevich/Shutterstock.com

Listen to ...

1. **"Not to be Believed"**

   Guest Storyteller: Brendan Bourque-Sheil,
   March 20, 2014

   Listen to this teller. He offers every emotion, picture, sensation, and tone imaginable. You will be listening to a star.

2. **"Eloquence and Professionalism"**

   Guest Storyteller: Elizabeth Ellis, May 29, 2014

   Listen to this famous teller and author and you will learn know why Elizabeth is considered one of the top storytellers in the nation. The stories she tells will forever be etched in your mind.

Understand

Symbol
Tools of speech
Variety of expression
Human senses
Story prop
Imagery

*"I want all my senses engaged.
Let me absorb the world's variety and uniqueness."*

—Maya Angelou

Symbolically Speaking

Language, nonverbal communication, and the construction of meaning are symbolic activities. In a story, words are used as symbols because they represent or stand for other things. Because symbols are arbitrary, they have no natural connection to what they represent until the communicator makes those symbols come to life through a variety of expressions.

You already know that symbolism can be an important feature in personal narratives. A storyteller may tell a tale about a vacant house on top of a hill to stand for his unattainable dream. Another might speak about a set of quilts seen at a bazaar to represent his intricate life. I remember one eloquent storyteller telling us about the most beautiful autumn day in Vermont she had ever seen. She spoke of a leaf clinging to a branch, when other leaves have fallen. Most of her story was spent describing this beautiful image. Then, almost in passing, she transitioned seamlessly to her father's battle with cancer and teased us by not offering closure to that part of the story. It became quite clear that her comprehensive description of the one remaining leaf was a symbol of hope for her father's survival. I was captivated by her use of symbolism. I felt fortunate to be a member of that audience.

Great storytellers use fascinating story symbols. Considered one of the greatest American novels, Harper Lee's *To Kill a Mockingbird* is often seen as a virtual clearinghouse of important story symbols. For instance, the brilliant relationships developed between characters clearly points to the mockingbird as a symbol of innocence and curiosity. Edgar Allen Poe's, "The Raven" is a symbol of the inevitable death of Virginia, Poe's beloved wife. As she suffers from consumption and awaits certain death, the Raven doggedly continues to tap on the chamber door, beckoning the protagonist to ask, "When will I see Lenore?" the Raven prognosticates, "Nevermore." Poe continues to asks his question vicariously (using the name, Lenore), and envisions her death more clearly each time the Raven utters, "Nevermore."

Symbols can intensify a story, encouraging an audience to search for meaning. Such intensity is also very common in children's stories, like those symbols used to convey the sadness of social disgrace we learn from Karen, the central character in Hans Christian Andersen's "The Red Shoes." Do you ever think about the symbols that repeat in different children's stories? Several stories take place in a castle. We find princesses locked in dungeons. And why is it so important to kiss so many princes? There are wicked witches, wicked stepsisters, wicked queens, and wicked parents. Deliciously inviting symbols, such as apples laced with poison, gingerbread houses enticing young children, and hens that lay golden eggs, all serve as an icon of danger and each is essential for understanding the intricate relationships between the characters, the plot, and the problem that the characters must solve.

Symbols used in a story force the storyteller to deliver language in meaningful, colorful, and descriptive ways. To warn your audience that you are about to tell "a sad story," does not make it so until you tell your story in a convincingly sad tone, assisted by the symbols used to highlight that sadness. Symbols allow us to name experiences and emotions, which is the primary way we give meaning to our lives. Because human beings are symbol "users," their uses of symbols are not confined to the here and now. Rather, symbols let us journey into the past (e.g., "I remember when I arrived at the restaurant"), future (e.g., "I will be there for your little league game . . . you can count on it"), and any dimension of time so that the designation of time differences infuse with the present.

Whether your story is about that argument you had with your father, your first bike, or "Pinocchio," a fundamental understanding of storytelling as a symbolic process can help you etch beautiful spoken images and successfully take an audience on a journey, and then return them safely to the present.

Economy of Words

Having a good sense of meaning of words is indispensable to a storyteller. A good sense of meaning of words implies that the teller has a good sense of meaning behind the symbols of a story. However, not commonly explored as a way to make words work well is the use of word economy. In short (not to make too fine a point), more words do not strengthen a story. In fact, an excess of words, especially fillers, or "segregates," such as, "you know, uh, like, and um" can severely cloud the meaning of a story, not to mention be a major distraction to the audience. On the other hand, some use of vocal fillers can restore a speech pattern belonging to one or more characters in a story. Read these two examples of the same message aloud, and sense how too many fillers can negatively influence the message, whereas a few strategically placed fillers can enhance the message:

It was like, I don't remember, you know? Like the first twenty or thirty, um, uh feet, you know, told me that as if it was like time to, you know, get ready for my like landing. To be like shot like from a cannon, you know, was like, I don't know, like unbelievable, you know?

Don't you dare tell me that the above illustration looks good to you. If it does, then I am especially glad you are taking this course. That illustration has a ridiculous amount of vocal fillers, and we all know there could have been more. This passage will illustrate a few carefully placed, *uh*, fillers:

I don't remember. The first twenty or thirty minutes warned me that it was time to prepare to land. You know, to be shot from a cannon was like, um . . . I don't know. It was just unbelievable.

Sometimes the best way to economize your word use is to use cryptic statements to replace sentences that are more tedious. This technique is not appropriate in written communication, because the rules are different. But when your story is designed to be spoken, your gestures, postures, eyes, face, and voice can more than compensate for the occasional use of cryptic thoughts. In fact, skillful delivery can make those cryptic thoughts quite powerful. Practice this segment. Read it aloud a few times. Do not add any words to it. What do you need to do with your face, voice, eyes, gestures, and postures to make it work?

Night. A cold night. Bitter, in fact. About 7:00. That call startled me. Startled me? Scared the hell out of me. I didn't expect it, you see. Well, not from her. No way hear from her, unless you expect to hear from a ghost. That's right, a ghost. So buckle up! This story is a ride, and I'll be taking you into dangerous traffic. No lights. No signs. No turning back.

With fewer words and a reduction of vocal fillers, consider how the use of the grammar in a story can help you to regulate the telling. In turn, your audience will become more attentive and attuned to what you want to achieve as a teller. Consider the following narrative segment by Rodney Orr, an electrician, telling his story about being bitten by a shark in a 2002 *Esquire* article entitled "What it Feels Like." Read it aloud and please follow these instructions: When you reach a comma, slowly say the letter, "A" silently to yourself. When you reach a period, slowly say, "AB." When you reach grammatical marks in this passage other than periods and commas, say "ABC." Try it.

"I swam back to my board. I was bleeding like hell, blood pouring out of my nose, out of my face. To escape a shark was nothing but luck. Nothing! Nothing could have saved me but luck! They took me away in the helicopter. I was taken to the hospital. Everyone looked at me as if I was hamburger. I still have some pretty bad scars on my face, but they fit in with my wrinkles."

Using vocal expression like the way a writer uses grammar is a principle we will revisit very shortly. But for now, could you feel the change in your rate of speech when reading the passage the way I asked? I bet you had plenty of energy and could read a complete sentence without running out of breath. I would also bet that the way you regulated the words and sentences helped to produce a change in the tension in the story. You can play with this technique and come up with a variety of configurations for regulating the rate (how quickly your words are spoken), pace (duration of story segments), and pauses (short, stretched, elongated) in a story, and ultimately help convey the tone of the story.

Storytellers who practice word economy tend to tell stories more effectively than tellers who use words excessively. Fewer vocal segregates, occasional cryptic thoughts, and rediscovering grammar as a way to regulate your spoken story can help make your story symbols more meaningful to your audience.

Tools of Speech

The magic of painting a spoken picture cannot be accomplished until the storyteller uses his speech tools successfully. These tools of speech include the tongue, teeth, lips, mouth, larynx, and diaphragm. These anatomical features work together to produce variations in sound. These variations are a direct result of how we use these tools to articulate and pronounce the words we need to convey. Articulation is the ability to pronounce the letters of a word correctly. Pronunciation is the ability to pronounce the entire word correctly. It is important in storytelling (and anytime you speak, unless you are intoxicated) to communicate letters and words clearly. However, there are times when experimenting with your speech tools can produce some creative results and convey a variety of images. These images can crystallize in the teller's mind and ultimately communicate them to listeners through a variety of expression.

Variety of Expression

Earlier in this book, I asserted that a good storyteller takes an audience on a journey and returns them safely to the present. This assertion suggests that oral performance is time-based. Listeners cannot go where they want when listening to a story. If the storyteller stops, the listeners must wait. If the teller speeds up, the listeners must catch up. An audience cannot take an orally presented story, shove it in a drawer, and read it again later. What helps the storyteller guide his listeners to where he wants to take them, while keeping them in the here and now, is an artful display of meaningful expression. A display of expression is crafted by the unique instruments of oral language, which include the use of voice, gestures (including face and posture), and eye contact.

Whether a variety of expression is used to tell an audience about a favorite camping trip, engage them in a favorite myth, or help them to uncover and rediscover the magical characters from a favorite children's story, each of these instruments allows the storyteller to convey meanings that, in written language, might need to be expressed primarily in words. So let's discuss these instruments and begin with the one the audience hears: the human voice.

Vocal Expression

When used correctly, the human voice should help an audience to listen carefully to *how* something *is* said, not *what* is said. This is called paralanguage. How would you know if someone is sarcastic when saying, "Oh, sure, I love liver and onions," "Of course I will love you forever," and "I can't wait to speak to you tonight"? What did you hear in your mind when depicting the sarcastic elements in the statements? Did you imagine a familiar tone, or "timbre"? Did voice inflections come to mind? Would the volume conveyed in the statements (loudly or softly) have any influence?

As you contemplate your responses to these admittedly simple questions, consider how difficult it would be for your listeners to make dozens of similar evaluations about a plethora of emotions in the story you tell, even a very short story, without your thoughtful and appropriate display of vocal variety. In the case of depicting sarcasm, you probably knew to listen for an inconsistency between the words and the tone. In that case, you would know to address the tone with your voice so that the "sarcastic" message is heard.

Storytelling requires that the teller use vocal variety to communicate many tones (mood of a story, the impression a teller wants to leave on the audience), images (the physical and aesthetic persona of the character and background), and emotions (responses felt and/or conveyed by story characters). The voice alone cannot communicate fully and completely all of the tones, images, and emotions in any story. It (the voice) needs help from other varieties of expression. But voice is essential. Let's explore more about vocal importance in storytelling by looking at tempo, rate, pitch, and volume.

If you are telling a story that includes a frustrated, demanding mother who is in the midst of reprimanding her daughter, a clear and even exaggerated, "I Said, No!" makes the point. But what if a character in your story is a little sloshed? Do not be using clear speech for this person. Slur your words, vary the tempo, vary the rate, think about your pitch, play with the volume, and do not sound articulate when painting the profile of your character in a drunken stupor.

Your vocal expression can also orchestrate the tempo, or "pace," by regulating the inherent rhythm of a story. Is the plot moving steadily, forging ahead with little or no detours? On the other hand, are there rifts and shifts that dart in and out of the story with a nervous frenzy? Thanks to our larynx and diaphragm, volume and projection also surface as useful for the storyteller. Volume refers to the loudness and softness of your voice, while projection refers to the depth and richness in your voice.

Try speaking directly from your throat, without taking a deep breath. Now as loudly as you can, say, "Welcome, all, and thank you for being here today." Was it a strain on your voice? That may be useful (for a very short time) if you are telling a story about the time you were screaming frantically at the pinch-hitter who came in at the bottom of the ninth inning, needing to score the runner on third to get your team into the World Series. Low volume can be useful when communicating the shy, reticent student who is terrified about giving his speech in front of the class for the first time. Low volume can compel your audience to lean forward as much as possible, as if to say, "Come on, you can do it."

Now, breathe deeply and try to use your gut rather than your throat, and repeat the earlier "Welcome . . ." line from above. Was there any difference? Was there less strain in your voice? You projected.

Projection is a product of good breathing. When you took that deep breath, you filled your diaphragm, a muscle that rests below your abdomen. Like a balloon, when you breathe correctly, your diaphragm is filled with plenty of air, allowing you to communicate with greater clarity and vocal richness. To be able to project will allow for those seated in the back of a room to hear your message. After all, when you tell us about the first time you told someone, "I love you," do you want it conveyed with loud throaty roughness, or with the sensual depth that comes from great projection?

Do you have a nervous character in your story? Try a higher pitched or fractured voice. Pitch is the highness or lowness of your voice. How about Charlie, the twelve-year-old seventh-grader smitten with Carla, the little girl who sits next to him in Social Studies? Charlie wants to sound more mature than he is, so give him the lower pitched voice. Add a comical topspin by fracturing his voice, thereby disclosing his true age.

Another use of vocal expression with a potentially entertaining effect is the intentional use of sound substitutions. Although never recommended in good written communication, a teller might want to use "budder" instead of butter (does the character have a cold?), "brute" instead of brewed (does the character tend to use malapropos?), "libary," not library (does the character have a tendency to speak unclearly?), and so on. Using substitutions can help you shape a number of different characters with an infinite combination of personalities, ages, education levels, and more.

Another kind of verbal substitution is the euphemism. I remember the time I interviewed a woman on the radio about the murder of her daughter. As you would imagine, it was an incomprehensible story. I was nervous. I wanted to say the right thing. I asked her to share the story of her daughter's untimely death with listeners and she said, "You mean when she was murdered?" It turned out this remarkable person who was about to convey the most difficult story any parent could possibly fathom preferred to use the word "murder" because she needed to hear it. And say it. For me, "untimely death" was a euphemism for murder. However, euphemisms can make stories somewhat hazy. Consider these examples of euphemisms:

Ethnic cleansing instead of genocide
Letting someone go instead of firing him
Correctional facility instead of jail
On the streets instead of homeless
Terminated pregnancy instead of abortion

As shown by these illustrations, euphemisms are polite expressions used in place of one that may be found offensive. These innocuous statements are quite appropriate in many situations, but using them in a story—particularly a personal story, may not meet a storyteller's needs. It did not in the case of the courageous mother to whom I earlier referred. The best advice is for storytellers to balance the need for certain descriptors with what listeners will hear comfortably when deciding on the best word to portray a potentially offensive behavior or circumstance.

Exploring Your Voice

There are several fun ways to practice the power of voice. Here is a variation of what researchers refer to as "content-free speech." Write several emotions, each on a separate index card. Without showing the emotion to your classmates, look at the index card given to you by your instructor, and think of a time when you felt that emotion. Then, by reciting the "ABCs," communicate the emotion clearly enough so that your classmates can guess what it is. Remember, you may only recite the "ABCs." Here are some good emotions to use:

Surprise
Fear
Anger
Happiness
Confusion
Anguish

Frustration
Jealousy

With the help of your classmates, discuss the exercise. What did you do with your voice to convey your emotion? What experience did you reconstruct in your mind to help you communicate the emotion? Which emotions were more difficult to identify? Other than your voice, what did you do to help convey the emotion? Were any of your expressions unplanned?

Using a suitable inflection, communicate each of these words. The sentence in parentheses suggests a specific meaning for the word, but do not read the sentence aloud. Just read the word. Concentrate.

So (*We've caught you, you rascal!*)
So (*What's it to you?*)
Stop (*I mean it!*)
Stop (*. . . in the name of the law!*)
Geez (*I lost a button!*)
Geez (*Are you kidding me?*)
Wow (*He/She is hot!*)
Wow (*I didn't think anyone could be that stupid!*)
Yes (*I'm sure!*)
Yes (*I think so*)

What did you think about before communicating the key word? Speaking of key words, how would you use your voice to emphasize the words in a sentence so that your audience can correctly interpret the meaning of that sentence? Read the following sentence and emphasize the word in caps:

YOU can't water those plants too much.
You CAN'T water those plants too much.
You can't WATER those plants too much.
You can't water THOSE plants too much.
You can't water those plants TOO much.

How did vocal emphasis change the meanings? The English language is difficult. One reason for that difficulty is that the same sentence with the same word can mean something entirely different when that word is emphasized. What you may have also noticed is that in most cases, the voice, as I suggested earlier, is not enough to give the listener an accurate interpretation. For example, in the fourth sentence in this exercise, it would have been very helpful if you gestured by pointing to the plants to which you referred.

Using your voice, or no voice, if you will, to pause at important moments in your story can effectively convey silence, movement, and stillness. Notice what happens when pauses are used in the following sentences. Read them aloud, and pause for two seconds when you see the bold "**P**."

My wife doesn't understand me. **P**. I'm not sure. **P**. Maybe she doesn't love me anymore.

No doubt I'm very **P** quiet. And I'm very pale. But yes. I am very **P** quiet.

I own this great Golden Retriever, Tim. He's like **P** Lassie. Remember **P** Lassie?

It was Jill. She **P** was the one. She was **P** the **P** one.

What did the pauses communicate about the speakers in those sentences? What was on their minds? What were they trying to convey to listeners? Under what circumstances can silence be effective?

Pauses are often viewed as a way a storyteller can create rhythm. Rhythm is a process by which listeners are led to listen to beats. Sentence variation is another rhythmic device because it can lead the attention of listeners to a designated set of words. Read these sentences aloud and feel the rhythm in each message.

She was right. Well, maybe she was, I think, but who really knows…Huh?

He saw. He left. He never went back.

Sylvia was one of those incredible, amazing, remarkable women who could drive any man wild. Except for me.

The human voice is indeed powerful. However, voice cannot stand alone. It needs help. So let us examine the other varieties of expression and build your expressive repertoire.

Expressive Movements

Kinesics (muscular movement) is the dimension of nonverbal communication that consists of gestures, such as hand movements and body shifts. Having said that, allow me to return to grammar for a moment. Earlier in this section, I touched on how looking at grammar in a cryptically conveyed story can help you regulate the telling more effectively. Just as punctuation marks can help you to regulate written messages, gestures can help you to regulate spoken ones. Say you want to convey one of your story characters asking a question. What do you do with your hands? That's an obvious one. But they get harder. How would you express passion? Rage? Anger? Surprise? Think of it this way. Since gestures work like grammar, what type of gesture would you use to communicate a comma, period, or exclamation mark?

Let's practice a bit. Get up. Get your hands out of your pocket. Read these sentences, sans grammar. Remembering that grammar regulates a message, decide what you want to communicate in the following statements. Adding what you have learned about voice, convey your messages with appropriate gestures.

Are you talking to me
I don't know why she swallowed the fly
Get away from me right now
I'm not to blame for your mistake
There is no way that could have happened
Take my word for it
There were several reasons we broke up such as a lack of affection attention and respect
That summer was the best ever it was serene and romantic

I picked her up at her house and was shocked to find her father answering the door
I never saw my father cry until that day that very moment

See how useful your gestures can be? It is impossible to imagine a good storyteller who has not mastered the use of gestures. To punctuate the point (yes, a pun is intended), no person in a straitjacket should pursue storytelling as a vocation.

Postural position can be a useful way to communicate the status or position of a story character, as well as help clarify his personality and emotions he needs to convey. Princes, paupers, rich, poor, strong, weak, meek, confident, passive, afraid, reluctant, and many more roles and adjectives illustrate the status or position held by a character, and they can be best conveyed through the clever use of postures. Experiment with postures that could be used to communicate the following descriptions:

He is a tower of strength.
He's a worm.
He stood proud and confident.
I heard some trepidation in his voice.
I was in awe of her.
I was embarrassed by the idea of asking her to dance.
Zeus was larger than the universe.
I looked up but couldn't see the stars.
I looked into the cave and saw utter darkness. It was a tiny crawl space.
I looked at my mother with newfound respect.

Postures and gestures can merge into open or closed positions, and can convey the degree of exposure to the world in which the storyteller is surrounded. Closed gestures and postures tend to protect the upper torso area. The shoulders, arms, and legs rotate "in." In the case of open gestures and postures, shoulders are back, palms face forward, and the legs are rotated "out." At a storytelling workshop, I remember a teller sharing the story of being in the hospital with a life-threatening disease. Once cured, this amazing teller wrapped his arms around his body as he described the blend of excitement and fear he felt when he did something as simple as taking a walk:

"I was so happy and so very afraid. I was dizzy with excitement and had to balance myself as I looked down and watched my feet take steps. I was in awe of everything around me. But really I was in awe because I couldn't believe I was alive. I was always tapping and poking some part of my body to check if I was here."

My impression was that the teller used closed postures and gestures to convey the emotional blending of wonder and disbelief he felt about being alive. When it was time for discussion, my impression was somewhat confirmed when I asked him "What prompted your choice of postures and gestures?" He answered, "I didn't know I was doing all that." After thinking a bit, he suggested that his partially conscious use of closed gestures and postures, culminating in the "hugging position" more fully described the strange internal contradiction between happiness and fear he felt at the time. After some more discussion, he disclosed, "I was terrified of the world and wanted to be within myself by myself. Then, I didn't. I couldn't decide."

The closed position isn't only helpful when telling a story of internal conflict; it can be an important addition to carving an image of a character, real or fictitious, who feels some reluctance, trepidation, uncertainty, or embarrassment about a situation he is about to confront. Remember when you were fourteen, wanting to ask Melanie to go to a movie? Were you not just a tad shy? What about fear of being rejected? Do you remember the positions of your posture and gestures at the time? Of course you don't. However, I can be fairly confident in guessing that there were no open postures or gestures at that moment for you, my friend.

Now since Paul Bunyan rode a big blue ox and had fists as big as choppin' blocks, I think we can safely say that he's an open posture and gesture kind of guy. If you are telling a tale about him, your gestures and postures had better show it. But you don't have to be Paul Bunyan to use an open position. Have you ever beaten the odds? Have you ever proved yourself victorious? How did you feel when you received an "A" on that exam for which you studied so hard? After saving for years to buy that vintage automobile, your discipline finally paid off. You finally quit smoking, and no one thought you could do it. You never thought you would ever again gain back your confidence after that terrible breakup. You feel proud, confident, strong, and independent, each conveyed by your open position asserting, "I have conquered it."

I have found that the use of both open and closed positions can be especially useful to the teller who wants to remain in a single space, or the teller who moves his feet very little to none at all. This type of storyteller is one whom I call a "purist," because he relies more heavily on himself in the storytelling process, as opposed to the "theatrical" teller who might move laterally and back and forth, and use a costume or elaborate prop in his telling. These types are a matter of taste, and both types are fine. However, and for what it is worth, most tellers are purists, and collectively endorse storytelling as a non-theatrical art. I am a purist, and I teach that style to my students. I ask students to either stand or to sit on a stool (for greater comfort and flexibility of movement) when telling their stories. I encourage the stool, because when their legs start a shakin' and their knees are a quakin' the "story stool" rules.

When seated, open and closed gestures and postures are excellent ways to compensate for not moving your feet. Moreover, open and closed positions can help a storyteller communicate distance. For example, a gentle lean forward closes the distance between the teller and listeners and can communicate interest ("Tell me more"), desire ("I need you so don't walk away"), and secrecy ("I want to let you in on a little secret"). Intimacy is a distance as well as feeling ("It's just you and me"), along with privacy ("Nothing is to go beyond this room, understand?"), all the while not moving your feet. Gently leaning back conveys feelings of disbelief ("I can't believe what you just said"), surprise ("Whoa, you are not what I expected"), and awe ("Oh, my, that is an incredible sight"). Scrunch down to "He's a worm," straighten up to "He's a tower of strength," open your palms to "The blazing sun," shrug those shoulders to

"They can say what they want," and stiffen your arm to tell me it is "Enough already!"

In Your Face

Great facial expression carries so much weight in storytelling that many tellers refer to storytelling as "Theater of the face." Think about it. Who can forget the mask in the film *Scream?* That face made an indelible impression on us, and the type of person behind that mask has caused many of our nightmares. The notorious mask in the movie is precisely the reason facial expression is so important to a teller.

For a storyteller, the face conveys the type of person in the story, along with the social role he plays. A social role is termed "persona," an Italian word that derives from the Latin, "mask" or "character." More specifically, in the study of communication, persona is a term given to describe versions, or multiple roles (personae) we play every day. In any given story, a teller must use his face to show the shifting of a character's persona. This shifting is seen whenever a character moves dramatically from one emotion to its opposite. For example, happy to sad, comedy to tragedy, despair to elation are common continua of emotions found in a plethora of stories.

The novel *American Psycho* by Brett Easton Ellis, also made into a movie, is the story of a successful Wall Street executive by day and very active sociopath by night. The novel points to the character's personae as the cause of his murderous tendencies. This story is an interesting illustration of how roles are morphed (inconspicuously blended, dissolved), and not a recommendation that we become psychopaths in order to use our face to convey various versions of a character. I would suspect that normal folk do facial morphing as much as the insidious characters found in scary stories.

To morph one's facial expression into the other is largely dependent on the teller's complete understanding of the version he wishes to show his audience. Try this. Look at the following set of sentences. Each set of two or three sentences will force a morphing of one facial expression into the other. These expressions are to be made without a break between them, in order to parallel the emotional circumstances they convey. So make a face, or two, or three. If you can do this in front of a classmate and keep a straight face ☺, so much the better for later discussion:

Sitting in a bar, waiting in anticipation:

Wow, I can't wait to meet him . . .

Oh, Hi, I didn't really recognize you.

Sitting in the waiting room to be interviewed for your first big job prospect:

I want this job so badly. But I am so mad at this guy. He told me to be here at 3:00 sharp, and now it's close to 4:00, and . . .

Hello, Mr. Dexter. No, I wasn't waiting too long. No problem.

Knocking at your grandmother's front door:

I can't believe I have to come here every Sunday afternoon . . .

Hi, Grandma. I'm so excited to see you again.

You are about to leave your house to go to your own wedding. You are to be married outdoors.

You open the door:

It's raining? Oh, My God, it's raining?

Thank goodness the sun looks as if it might sneak through. Oh, please, please, please . . .

The sun is out, yes, yes, yes, yes, yes . . .

Go away cloud. A cluster of clouds? Where did they come from? More clouds. Oh, no!

How did your facial expression shift along with the changes in your feelings? What kind of feelings prompted certain physical features on your face to change? Try this exercise in front of a mirror at home the next time you rehearse a story. In addition, storytellers contend that stretching your facial muscles so that expressions can be exaggerated a bit (think amplification) is important so that the audience can clearly see, and feel, the persona behind it. Since eyes are found in the face, it makes sense to continue our facial expressions by adding eyes to this discussion.

Hey, "Look me in the eyes and say that," is a line as common as brushing your teeth in the morning. And it should be. In most cultures, eye contact is an important element of nonverbal communication. In dialogue, too much eye contact can be intimidating for some, and too little is too distant for most. Just the right amount of eye contact can get others involved in your message. In public speaking, a speaker should look at his audience rather than focus on that single friendly face, or on an imaginary dot on the back wall. Just as eye contact is important to a public speaker or anyone involved in a dialogue, making eye contact with listeners is crucial for a storyteller. Among other things, eye contact is a way for a teller to establish rapport with his audience, as well as equalize the status of the relationship between himself and his listeners.

In their book, *The Power of Story: Teaching through Storytelling*, Pamela Cooper and Rivas Collins contend, "Unlike theater, in which actors usually don't acknowledge the presence of the audience, storytellers speak directly to their listeners." These authors view eye contact as the most viable way to establish this presence with the audience. In turn, this presence helps to create a private, rather than public relationship with the listeners. This privacy between teller and listeners is what professional storyteller and educator Lynne Rubright refers to as the moment when storytelling becomes a "poetically intimate art form that exists eye to eye and heart to heart."

Borrowing from Cooper and Collins, I found that exploring eye contact in terms of "circle of awareness" is quite useful when making decisions about ways to connect an audience to story characters. In the first circle, the storyteller is self-contained and communicates the inner feelings of the character (real or fictitious).

In this case, eye contact may not be made with the audience at all, or if it is, it is very limited. Still, the audience is present, as if they are eavesdropping on the teller talking to himself. For example, the audience is not present when Hamlet contemplates suicide with "To be or not to be. That is the question." That is a soliloquy, much as we do when we are alone, talking to ourselves. No one is invited to listen. When telling a story, the physical audience is invited. However, like Hamlet, we use creative eye contact to communicate to our listeners that they are not supposed to be there. We might look at the ceiling, or somewhere else away from the audience. If communicating despair or desperation, we might stare at the ground.

In the second circle, the storyteller may need to keep eye contact with an imaginary character while having a dialogue with him. When Peter Pan says to Tink, "You drank my poison, didn't you?" Peter speaks to the light, a definite focal point so that the audience knows where Tinkerbell is located. You expect your sister, Jill, to be home soon. You hear your front door open. No one speaks and the lights are out. You can't see a thing. It's probably your sister, so you turn toward the door and ask, "Jill, is that you?" Will your audience know where the door is located? What will you do with your eyes when you follow the person walking across the room?

The third and fourth circles of awareness consider the very real audience. The third circle will create the intimate relationship with your audience that you may require. It is most useful when speaking directly to a very real person, such as in a personal narrative. If you are speaking to your father, you may look directly at someone in your audience. To increase the involvement of your listeners, you might even look at someone different each time you speak to your father. You would make the same eye contact when addressing other characters in your narrative. Although it will not create the intense intimacy as the third circle, the fourth circle of awareness can involve the entire audience. However, you may not want that level of intimacy with them because of the sensitive subject matter in your story. In this case, it might be best to look at clusters of listeners, perhaps five or six for about five or six seconds.

Although most tellers commit to a consistent form of eye contact when sharing a story, a blend of eye contact can be useful when guiding an audience through a maze of both real and fictitious characters, as well as a way to convey different points of view (first, third person) within a given story.

Most storytellers will never need to worry about this complex configuration of matching eye contact with points of view to real or fictitious characters. However, it is also important to appreciate how this challenging blend of eye contact, point of view, and character type can work almost effortlessly in some of our favorite classic stories. In James Joyce's *Ulysses*, there can be found instances of direct first person, followed by third person narration mixed with first person stream of consciousness, and finally the famous extended, reflective first person soliloquy that ends the story. I have watched professional storytellers, actors, and readers perform parts of this novel. In every case, the successful performer used the circles of awareness, consistent with how he wanted to involve the audience.

Clearly, our face and eyes convey a wide range of feelings and emotions. The feelings and emotions of any character cannot be completely communicated through facial expressions and eye contact alone. In fact, to convey a full slate of feelings and emotions requires that the teller draw from a full variety of expression. When artfully used by the storyteller, this variety of expression can create memorable images for any audience.

Imagine That!

Storyteller Jay O'Callahan points to the storyteller's ability to visualize and create images to be at the very heart of storytelling. This is an important point, because a good storyteller is only equipped to transfer images to his audience by first creating those images in his own mind. Haley Joel Osment did this a little too effectively in the film *Sixth Sense*, when he declared, "I see dead people." I do not think we want to be that convincing. Nevertheless, as storytellers, we do want to benefit from the power of imagery.

Images are those pictures we paint for our listeners with a variety of expression, and imagery is the formation of those images in our minds. Let us try some imagery by internalizing a series of character traits, and then use a variety of expression to create images of those traits. Think about the three witches in *Macbeth*. You have read *Macbeth*, right? At the outset of this masterpiece, three witches await the Thane of Glamis and say:

Witch #1: "When shall we three meet again, in thunder, lightening, or in rain?"

Witch #2: "When the hurly-burly's done. When the battle's lost and won."

Witch #3: "That will be ere the set of sun."

Witch #1: "Where the place?"

Witch #2: "Upon the heath, there to meet with Macbeth . . . ."

Get one of your classmates to speak these lines. With your eyes shut, have your peer recite these lines without any vocal changes. You should be asking yourself, "Which witch is which?" Next, have your classmate use vocal variety to distinguish between the witches. Unless your contemporary hasn't the foggiest idea of how a witch sounds, the delineation should now be clear. Now open your eyes and have your classmate add gestures, postures, and colorful facial expressions for each witch. The witches should then appear (sort of) in front of your eyes in their entire spooky splendor. When you see these witches emerge in front of you, it is because the classmate teller successfully created the image of each of the ugly old hags. Even the setting can help a teller internalize the mood of the scene. Let's crank this exercise up a notch. Scan this partial list of categorical characteristics of the witches.

Voices

Crackly
Rough
High pitched
Medium pitched

Low pitched
Hoarse
Nasal
Scary
Wicked

Postures

Hunched over
Rounded shoulders
Stooped down
Close together

Gestures

Hands circling cauldron with large spoon in hand
Laughing
Glaring eyes
Moving long fingers with sharp nails

Descriptors/Adjectives

Confident
Tall hats
Ugly
Old
Green
Stringy hair
Long nose
Warts
Black eyes
Tall hats

Context

Forest
Dark
Owls

Crickets
Fire
Cave

I have a hunch you know what follows. Three of you at a time will become these three witches. Don't worry. No one is watching. Shut the door to your classroom and do it. First, internalize the descriptors/adjectives (imagery) you see above. Next, decide what vocal characteristics, posture and gestures, facial expression, and eye contact each of you will use to convey your designated "witchy" image. After each frightening trio has done their thing, discuss it as a class. Go to the next trio, discuss, and repeat until every trio had their fun. Discuss the variations in expression used by the witches in each trio. Which ones were especially effective? How did the choices in expression help the trio interact with each other?

Now let me add an ingredient to the image-building recipe with a hearty dose of our sensations. You know what they are: touch (tactile), sight (visual), smell (olfactory), aural (hear), and taste (gustatory). For extra flavor, we will throw in a dollop of movement (kinesthetic). You will now be able to use your palette of expression to paint images with a heightened level of clarity, thanks to the addition of your five senses plus one. Recite these lines. Use a comprehensive set of expression to paint the spoken pictures in these sentences. Exaggerate your gestures, postures, face, eyes, and voice to feel the picture you are painting so clearly:

Tactile

"He brushed against me because he wanted my attention."
"Oh, that kiss was, well . . . it just worked."
"Pushing my way through the crowd on Times Square was scary."

Visual

"Now that's a gorgeous woman."
"That guy's a model? Are you kidding me?"
"The desert at night is made of colors not possible to describe."

Olfactory

"The stench of garbage was all over the house."

"Wait. I think something is burning. Is that dinner? Is that your roast burning?"

"Cinnamon rolls. I love cinnamon rolls . . . fresh, warm cinnamon rolls."

Aural

"Ask not for whom the bell tolls; it tolls for thee."

"Lower your voice. I said lower it. You'll wake the baby."

"Did you hear that? Listen. It's faint but clear. Listen!"

Gustatory

"Yuck. How long has the coffee been on?"

"I ate raw oysters for the first time and they were, well, hard to swallow."

"A mild jalapeno? Are you kidding me? Water. Ice water. Lots of ice. Water. Beer. Hurry!"

Kinesthetic

"My arm is so stiff it feels like I have arthritis."

"I'm moving this way because I'm sunburned. Can't you see?"

"I can't see the top of the building."

How did you do? It isn't easy, is it? Adding sensory discoveries to our images requires a great deal of concentration. So concentrate. Break up into pairs. Imagine there is an apple tree in front of you. One at a time and without a sound, fluidly show your partner the following three actions in this order: (1) How difficult or easy it is to pull the apple off the tree. (2) The size of the apple. (3) What does the apple taste like? Watch your partner carefully. Talk about the experience.

Was there tension in his shoulders to show how difficult it was to pull the apple from the tree? When he grabbed the apple, did his palm remain open? After all, it wasn't the incredible shrinking apple. Unless it's a tree that grows magical fruit (possible in a fantasy or fairy tale), an apple does not change its size or shape. So why move your palm while you hold the apple in it? When your partner bit into the apple, could you tell if it was sweet or sour? Sensory discovery using gestures, postures, face, and eyes is a broad stroke toward achieving storytelling excellence.

Using your skills in expression, imagery, and sensory discovery, practice communicating these two passages, one taken from a narrative delivered by one of my students, and one from the 1890 popularized version of "Jack and the Beanstalk" by Joseph Jacobs. I realize you do not own the narrative, so expressing it the way its teller would convey it isn't to be expected. The story is not familiar to you. However, if you hadn't been exposed to Jack most of your life, would he be familiar to you? Try to feel these two different messages and give them a shot.

"Eventually my mother left my dad. The apartment we moved to seemed smaller than the walk-in closet in my old room. I couldn't move without running into my mother and two younger brothers. What made things worse was that my mother smoked. She tried to quit but the tension and pressure didn't let her. I choked every night. One night I told her she was being selfish. She yelled at me. She slapped me. She threw a magazine at me. She never did any of that before. My brothers cried all night. We had no money. She didn't have a job, but was out looking for one every day. I worked at a boutique three days a week, then ran home to make dinner. I usually burned everything in sight. If I didn't burn it, it was too salty or had no taste or whatever."

"As Jack slept, the beans grew in the soil, and the gigantic beanstalk grew in their place by morning. When Jack saw the huge beanstalk, he immediately decided to climb, climb, and climb, until he arrived in a land far above the clouds. This land happened to be the home of a giant. The house was bigger than the land from where Jack came. He broke into the giant's house, for the giant had many

treasures. Jack tried to hide, thanks to the help of the giant's wife. But the giant knew Jack was near and said:

"Fi-fi-fo-fum
I smell the blood of an Englishman
Be he live or be he dead
I'll grind his bones to make my bread."

With imagery and a treasure chest of expression, the storyteller uses both broad and finer strokes to paint spoken pictures of real and imaginary life, so that the wonder of a story can unfold like a well-worn magic carpet, and carry its travelers to places they have never been, and into worlds that enrich their lives.

Show and Tell

Do you remember "Show and Tell"? Just as it was fun and meaningful to talk about an object of personal importance and show it to your classmates at the same time, it can be fun and meaningful to use props when telling a story. Common storytelling props include puppets, costumes, musical instruments, toys, picture books, personal heirlooms, and other personal items. Admittedly, I do not use props very often. Still there are times when using a prop is not only appropriate, but if used effectively, can mesmerize an audience. I have observed my storytelling friend use puppets when telling "Where the Wild Things Are" by Maurice Sendak, with enormous success to his very young audiences. His timing is impeccable and his skills extraordinary.

One occasion when I do use a prop is when I tell the story of the "Gingerbread Man" to a young audience. I use a toy called a limber-Jack (a refined wooden man, simple in design, who sits on a wooden plank that rests on your knees and when a teller taps the plank, the wooden man dances around). When I arrive at the chorus, "Run, run, run, just as fast as you can, but you won't catch me 'cause I'm the Gingerbread Man," I manipulate the little wooden man so he dances to the rhythm of the tapping of the plank. The little dance prompts my young listeners to repeat those lines, and gives me a chance to interact with them during the story.

I need to qualify something here. I do not mesmerize an audience. I'm not that good with props, but I'm working on it. I have a hard enough time telling a good story all by my lonesome. In addition, for those of you who care, you can purchase a limber-Jill to go with your limber-Jack, and practice your conversations with dates or your partner ☺. But good luck in trying to use both the limber guy and gal in the same story. That would be a real knee-slapper! Sorry. I had to say it.

Having said that, let me make it clear that a prop should never be difficult to handle. In addition, a prop should not require you to move around very much. Cumbersome props that encourage too much movement or theatrics can quickly detach you from your audience and shift your program from storytelling to a bad one-person theater production. Instead, the teller should effortlessly manipulate a prop so that it becomes a seamless addition to the story itself. If you choose to use a prop, be sure to include it when rehearsing your story. You may think you know exactly how it will fit in, but if you are the least bit uncomfortable, it will detract the audience from listening to your story.

If you think that props are best suited for a younger audience, you would be correct. For many children's storytellers, props can highlight a cultural ritual, teach a song, compare and contrast social mores between communities, and fuel an interactive energy between themselves and their young listeners. However, a prop can also be useful when telling a personal narrative to an adult audience. Think about the beautiful story about Grandpa's watch, Mother's first doll, that empty frame in which your firstborn's picture will be placed, the hat donned by Uncle Sid when he reached Ellis Island, family awards, special heirlooms, private trinkets, and more. Briefly showing these kinds of items from which your story evolved can give it a deeply captivating and sentimental flavor, bringing your listeners even closer to you. Regardless of the prop, it should be used only to enhance your story, or as the title of this chapter proclaims, another way to paint your spoken picture.

Final Remarks...

As you continue to assemble a range of human expression, you will find that your ability to confront a myriad of story images and paint them with your voice, eyes, face, gestures, and postures is well within your reach. In turn, those images will transform into an appealing sensory experience for all to enjoy.

"I eat my peas with honey,
I've done it all my life . . .
It makes them taste so funny . . .
But it keeps them on my knife."

—Children's Rhyme

Chapter 8

Learning to Tell a Story

Listen to ...

1. **"House of Pies"**

   Guest Storyteller: Katie Galloway, November 21, 2013

   Listen to the reason Katie received more responses from her story than any other teller . . . including the pros. Pies, sexual assault, and brother's death . . . all done with humor and optimism and by learning her "most important thing." She redefined awesome.

2. **"How to Lie"**

   Guest Storyteller: Sheila Starks Phillips, April 3, 2014

   Listen to Sheila, a Houston Storyteller's Guild Liar Contest champion, lie like a bandit . . . and teach us all how to do it. It's about fun, fun, fun . . . and some intense sequencing.

Understand

Sequencing
Rhythm
MIT
Story boards
Competencies

*"There is only one love—and Stories.
All else is but a shadow dream."*

—*Vera Nazarian*

Oh, Yes. I Remember

The snow blanketed the . . . the . . . the . . . um, uh, oh yeah, blanketed the road causing our travel to be . . . be . . . be . . . crippled. Yeah, crippled. Then, I clawed my way to . . . to . . . to . . . (I knew it this morning), to . . . to . . .

Did you forget something? The words? What you forgot was to learn the story. Memorizing words will not provide you with control of the story, not to mention control over how your audience will respond to it. This is not to say that memorization has no role in learning a story. Some rote memorization can be helpful. For example, repeated refrains are best memorized (*"Little Pig, Little Pig, let me in! Not by the hair on my chinny chin chin"*). Garrison Keillor claims that the smartest thing he ever did as a teller was to memorize the beginning and ending of a story. For Keillor, this method allows him to enter the world of the story as if he lived it.

Garrison Keillor is more famous than any teller in modern time is, so he will get no argument from me. The main thing to remember is that learning a story does not require rote memorization of the words in the story. That process will almost certainly yield the paralyzing results to which I referred at the beginning of this section. Besides, the more you practice your story aloud, the more you will naturally remember it. Let's take this a little further.

We have all heard hilarious jokes. Have you ever tried to repeat that hilarious joke to a friend, only to find your friend not laughing? You used almost the same words conveyed in the joke that had you in stitches. Again, the words remembered aren't nearly enough. You need to tell the joke many times to acquire the right timing, vocal cadence, and ways to deliver the punch line. Learning a story requires the same level of practice. As long as the integrity of a story is maintained, using comfortable words that work well in conveying the story is fine. This principle is clearly applied to folktales and fables. These stories, after all, are brewed and blended over time. One version of Aesop's "The Lion, The Mouse, and The Fox" begins:

A lion was lying asleep at the mouth of his den when a mouse ran over his back and tickled him so that he woke up with a start and began looking about everywhere to see what it was that had disturbed him.

It might be more comfortable to say,

A lion was fast asleep in his den. Just then a mouse scampered across his back, tickling the lounging lion. The lion was startled and suddenly awoke; looking around feverishly to determine what disturbed him.

You don't care for this version? Create your own. Retelling a story in your own words and keeping the honor of that story is easy if you know the story. Knowing a story means you learned it well and preserved its core. Many storytellers would say you tamed your tale.

So let us examine some simple methods for learning, or "taming," a story so that you can get comfortable with the stories you tell. Why tame your tale? "Because wild thing, you make my heart sing." As the song continues, we learn that "Wild thing, I think you move me. But I want to know for sure . . ." Stories we begin to learn are wild and baffling at first. Cooper and Collins in their chapter "Taming Stories for Telling" from *The Power of Story* are far more eloquent:

"Perhaps there is a story, ancient or new, waiting for you to make ties, inviting you to become unique to each other. To share the story with others, you must spend time with it first. Perhaps there is a story, still slightly wild, whose eyes are trying to say, 'If you please . . . tame me.'"

When repeatedly telling an informal personal narrative or, in the case of someone else's story, reading it a few times, a teller develops what Doug Lipman calls an unconscious conception of its structure, such as where the climaxes occur and how each element in the story relates to each other. Once you obtain this loose conception of the story, it is easier to place the story in an outline, tailored to represent your concept of the story's structure.

An outline works for the teller the same as a blueprint would to an architect. The blueprint is simply a model of a home, just as an outline is a model of your story. There is no wit, humor, passion, or any emotion in either an outline or a blueprint. The blueprint consists of lines, shapes, and numbers, and the outline is a series of declarative statements. Both a house and story come to life because of the people who inhabit them. With this analogy in mind, let us explore the idea of story sequencing.

Order, Order, Order

Learning the sequence of events in a story is a logical place to begin and can be a very effective type of outline. Sequencing is key to outlining and is accomplished a number of ways. Some storytellers will group incidents into the beginning (setting the plot, characters), middle (complications rising, conflicts, tensions), and end (resolution), not unlike the way a speech is crafted. This type of sequencing is helpful in learning several kinds of stories, particularly those with lots of detail.

Sequencing encourages the teller to think coherently about the story. Moreover, it helps the teller feel comfortable about using a variety of words that will keep the integrity of the story intact, while reducing the anxiety that comes with the fear of forgetting specific words. Since sequencing is a technique used to rehearse a story, the way a story is sequenced need only to make sense to the teller who designs it. Ultimately, sequencing is a creative way for a storyteller to learn and control his story.

One way to demonstrate the power of sequencing is to practice it in class. A popular method is for one student to begin a story with an impromptu opening. Then stop after a few moments. The next student, designated by the instructor based on where he is seated in the room or by some other method, continues the story until told to stop (*usually by the instructor or the student who began the story*). This continues until the last student in the room finishes the story. Each student must listen to each other in order to convey a segment that coherently follows what was just heard. Making sense of a story as a class can be a powerful exercise in sequencing. You can begin a story with anything and in any way:

Once upon a time, there was a very young rooster . . . **Stop!** *Someone continues . . .*

One day, my cousin, Teddy said . . . **Stop!** *Someone continues . . .*

I walked up the hill and saw the alleged haunted house . . . **Stop!** *Someone continues . . .*

Get the idea? Good. Try your own.

I often use this exercise successfully in my own class. I also use several published short stories to conduct the same exercise. This variation will help you learn a story that isn't yours. Most recently, I used "An Occurrence at Owl Creek Bridge" by Ambrose Bierce. First, I show this wonderfully haunting Civil War tale in its film form, first shown in February 1964 as an episode of the *Twilight Zone*, hosted by master storyteller, Rod Serling. I show this riveting story one time to my class before I take them to the sequencing exercise designed to retell it. I will begin with some sort of prologue. Then, I will ask a student to begin telling the actual story, directing him to use first or third person as my only instruction.

Because my storytelling class is seated in a circle, I simply say, "Stop," after ninety seconds or so, and ask the next student in the circle to continue the story. When we reach the second-to-last student, I will ask that student to begin to wrap up the story, before the final student brings the story to closure. Here is an example of a prologue I might use to begin the exercise:

Often our lives rotate like a kaleidoscope, complete with stark changes in shapes and colors. Sometimes, this human rotation is far too rapid for complete comprehension, especially when seen through the eyes of a doomed confederate soldier in "An Occurrence at Owl Creek Bridge," by Ambrose Bierce.

We repeat this exercise a few times, each time with a different student introducing it with his own prologue. It is amazing at how well the class learns to tell (*sequence*) a story together after seeing it only once. However, they tell it several times. What they do to help each other is precisely what good storytellers do by themselves, that being to think in sequences and practice the story often.

Another useful exercise in sequencing is to place a list of random details in order. Sometimes the easiest thing to do when learning a story is to list the details to be included in your story without concern for the order in which they took place. Say, for instance, the following list of details is important to the story you wish to construct. In what order would you place these so that they are sequenced appropriately? Place the correct number next to the detail. Try it.

___ He was mad

___ He sped down the street

___ He ran out of the house

___ He got into his car

___ He explained how angry he was at his daughter

___ He rolled down the window

___ He hit a parked car

___ He slammed the car door behind him

___ You could hear him yelling a mile away

___ Officers got to the accident scene

How did you do? The first two details are interchangeable. After that the sequence is well defined.

Considering the natural sequence of numbers found in so many children's stories (e.g., "Three Little Pigs," "Three Billy Goats Gruff," "Goldilocks and the Three Bears,"), sequencing by numbers can be an effective strategy for learning a children's story (*How does the Troll respond to the first, second, and third Billy Goat?*).

Other tellers create a storyboard in which a series of pictures illustrate the story. Because children's stories are pictorial, learning a story picture-by-picture can be helpful. I cannot draw, but if I could, I would draw pictures of the characters in "Jack and the Beanstalk" (or any children's story) in the order they appear in the story. A way to try this method is to read a fable (it's short and pictorial) aloud in class. Identify someone who can sketch the story's characters, setting, and so forth in the order they appear in the story. The person who reads the story and the one who draws it operate simultaneously. The drawings must be visible to everyone in class. After the fable is read (and drawings completed), conduct an exercise like the one used for the *Twilight Zone* episode. But this time use the drawings, not words.

The first student starts by looking at the first sketch and using it to recall how the story begins. When the next student hears "Stop," he ponders the next sketch and continues the story, and so forth. This technique for learning a story is not appealing for everyone, even for those whose stories are "picture perfect" and therefore conducive to the method. It is a good option for those who are extremely visual and like to tap into their improvisational skills. However, even the most visually minded teller who finds it easy to learn a story by sketching a cow, a beanstalk, a giant, and a golden egg may be hard-pressed to use drawings to learn the story about the time his Uncle Al won a spaghetti-eating contest.

Another form of learning a story is a memory graphic. Similar to a storyboard, a memory graphic is a road map of sorts, helping a teller to see the story in its entirety. But unlike the pictorial storyboard, this graphic might include bibliographic details, plot synopsis, story opening, characteristic phrases (devices of repetition, characteristic voices, and individual personalities), story closure, action spirals, and more. This type of graphic might be a better choice for learning that story about Uncle Al. But if you want to draw pictures to help you remember Uncle Al, go for it! The choice of technique is yours, and that choice should facilitate your way of thinking.

Storyboards with pictorial graphics and memory graphics are akin to sequencing because they assist the teller in thoroughly remembering the story, and by encouraging the teller to think about the chronology of the story and to prepare accordingly. Again, choosing the sequencing technique from which you will learn the story is up to you. So use what works best to tame your tale.

Feel the Rhythm

I love nursery rhymes. "Old Mother Hubbard," "The Cow that Jumped Over the Moon," "Wee Willy Winkie," "Humpty Dumpty," "Jack and Jill," "Jack be Nimble." Remember Jack Sprat?

Jack Sprat could eat no fat; his wife could eat no lean. And so betwixt them both, they licked the platter clean.

"Remember" is indeed the operative word. We remember them because we remember the rhythmic features that create them. Like nursery rhymes, an abundance of fairy tales, folktales, and fables, especially those written for children, are also rhythmic and for very good reason: rhythm helps a child acquire language skills. Keeping this in mind, a storyteller can more easily learn to tell a rhythmically rich story by having a better understanding of how children learn language through rhythm.

A child's language skills are directly related to the number of words and complex conversations they have with others. In order to learn the relationship between sounds and objects, a child must hear the sounds, and then make the association between the sound and what it symbolizes. By repeating those sounds and objects, rhythm makes this association possible. By combining sequencing (e.g., "The Cat in the Hat" *balances a cup, milk, cake, three books, the fish, a rake, a toy boat . . .*) with phonetic awareness (letter familiarity), rhythm helps a storyteller to recognize language patterns and predict language outcomes much the same way a child learns language. How do you think Maria taught the Von Trapp children to read music? What am I talking about? Immediately rent *The Sound of Music* and feel embarrassed. Be very embarrassed.

Okay, let's predict a few outcomes. Please fill in these blanks:

"Cats here, cats there,
cats and kittens _____"

"Sylvester McMonkey McBean
had them walk through his Star-Off _____"

Big Bad Bill bought Bull Bob a Beer,
then Big Bad's wife said, "Come along my _____"

Skinny and Fatty went to bed,
when Fatty rolled over, Skinny was _____

You should have had an easy time coming up with not only a rhyming word, but also the word that fit the phrase (I made two of them up). Would you say, " . . . Skinny was red?" I hope not. It wouldn't fit. Predicting language outcomes by examining the rhythmic patterns in a story can be a fun and effective way to learn a story.

See how quickly you learn the following rhyme by hearing (and feeling) the rhythm. Time yourself. You will be impressed at how little time it took for you to learn it.

Snakes and cakes and pumpkin pie
Oldest sister, you can't fly.
Salt and pepper, bouncing ball
Middle sister, you will fall.
Oldest sister, you can fly
All you have to do is try
Middle sister, flying's fun

The spell I made is now undone.
So feel the rhythm, feel the beat

Nod your head and tap your feet.
Learn the rhythm, each meter and rhyme
Now tell your story. It's about that time.

Now get out there and tell "Yertle the Turtle" with confidence.

The Important Thing Is

Determining the MIT (Most Important Thing) is an approach to learning a story best suited for the seasoned teller. This principle, first coined by Doug Lipman, is deceptively challenging because of its metaphysical nature, meaning the teller cannot always articulate the way he used the MIT to learn his story. I know this sounds confusing, but maybe this will help. There are times when you need nothing more than grit and determination to get something done. You want to get it done so badly that you find a way to achieve it. Sometimes you don't know how you did it. In fact, if a friend asked, "How did you do it?" you might find your only response to be, "I don't know. I just did it."

MIT works in a similar way because some storytellers require nothing more than their drive and motivation to tell their stories. I want to be clear in telling you that you can be intensely motivated to tell your story and find that this metaphysical approach is useless to you. That is perfectly all right. This is just an option. If it sounds like an option, then please keep reading. Whether the story you choose to tell originates with you or someone else, list on a sheet of paper all the reasons you have for telling the story. Take your time and be as comprehensive with your list as you can. When you have finished your list of reasons, examine it and determine the most important reason for telling the story. What you select is your MIT. The Most Important Thing could be:

What do you love most about the story?
What draws you to the story?

What is the story about for you?
How does the story make you feel?
What prompted you to want to tell the story?
What does the story mean to you?
What do you want to communicate through the story?
How do you want your audience to react to your story?

Once you think about your MIT, the rest of the story should theoretically fall naturally into place for you. The notion is that you are now so excited, passionate, and involved in your story that you would not dare risk losing the attention of your listeners by delivering it poorly. Tellers who use the MIT method claim that it helps them to make their own interpretations of events and ideas available to others.

MIT can be described as a procedure when a teller focuses on a single symbol, usually an heirloom or piece of memorabilia. The teller then uses that symbol to resuscitate the complete story that surrounds it. Jay, a friend and colleague, uses MIT to tell a wonderful story about his mother's last Christmas. Let me paraphrase:

Every Christmas morning, my brothers and I sat under the tree patiently waiting for our mother to walk around the corner of the kitchen, holding her favorite coffee cup, and come into the living room and take a seat on the same spot on the sofa, balancing her cup of coffee. Then, with her signature smile, she gave us permission to open our gifts. She watched as we ripped open our presents. Then, she would smile and look at us in a way that would always proclaim, "You boys make me so happy." But on her last Christmas my brothers and I did not rip open our presents. We opened them slowly because we wanted that Christmas, my mother's last Christmas, to last forever.

Jay shared this tender story during one of the holiday programs on my radio show. When I asked, "What allows you to remember this story so vividly" he answered, "I see my mother holding her coffee cup. I hone in on that cup. That's all I need to make the story come to life." Mom's coffee cup is Jay's MIT.

One of the stories I ask you to examine in this chapter is the riveting account told by Katie Galloway, one of the most courageous storytellers I have ever had the good fortune to meet. She will take you on an intense and vivid excursion to her sexual assault, her brother's death, and eating the best slice of pie in the world. Don't try to make meaning from these seemingly unrelated events, because Katie does it brilliantly thanks to her unlikely MIT: A menu. Listen to her story and answer these questions:

How many emotional shifts did you depict in her story?

How did Katie help you to return to her MIT as the code that held the story together?

It should be no surprise that the MIT technique can also be used to learn traditional stories. Try the MIT principle on "King Midas." Read the story. Then, decide what about the story is most important to you. Try to retell the story using your MIT as your incentive.

King Midas was a very kind man who ruled his kingdom fairly, but he was not one to think very deeply about what he said. One day, while walking in his garden, he saw an elderly satyr asleep in the flowers. Taking pity on the old fellow, King Midas let him go without punishment. When the god Dionysus heard about it, he rewarded King Midas by granting him one wish. The king thought about it for only a few seconds and then said, "I wish for everything I touch to turn to gold." And so it was.

The beautiful flowers in his garden turned toward the sun for light, but when Midas approached and touched them, they stood rigid and gold. The king grew hungry and thin, for each time he tried to eat, he found that his meal had turned to gold. His lovely daughter, at his loving touch, turned hard and fast to gold. His water, his bed, his clothes, his friends, and eventually the whole palace were gold.

King Midas saw that soon his whole kingdom would turn to gold unless he did something about it. He asked Dionysus to turn everything back the way it was and take back his golden touch.

Because the king was ashamed and very sad, Dionysus took pity on him and granted his request. Instantly, King Midas was poorer than he had been, but richer, he felt, in the things that mattered most.

Jot down the single Most Important Thing for you in the story.

The MIT: _____

Now, concentrate on that single important thing and without looking at the story a second time, tell the story aloud. Improvise and do the best you can. Remember to concentrate on clearly communicating your MIT to your audience.

How did you do? How did you get to your MIT? How successful were you at improvising portions of the story? For continued practice, try a personal story using the same instructions you followed for King Midas. Repeat the discussion questions.

Your MIT for any story may remain the same, or it may change over time. Whatever the case or however you approach it, your MIT for a story can be an invaluable guide to the many decisions you make about learning and telling your story.

Working a Checklist

I think it is wise to have a checklist of important decisions you need to make, and learn, in order to tell your story well. Before every assignment, I provide my students with the same rubric I will use to evaluate that assignment. I suggest they use the evaluation forms when rehearsing and to treat each like a checklist for that assignment. I use several forms, but here are two: the narrative and folktale/fable assignments. These rubrics identify the basic competencies I ask students to master. Regardless of how your own instructors evaluate you, you cannot go wrong by trying to ace these competencies. I hope this helps.

PERSONAL NARRATIVE:

1 point = unsatisfactory
2 points = satisfactory
3 points = excellent

Competency 1
Effectiveness of prologue ____

Competency 2
Focused episode clearly conveyed ____

Competency 3
Audience clearly defined and addressed ____

Competency 4
Tone communicates interest ____

Competency 5
*Fluid sequencing, meaningful transitions
designed to connect thoughts and ideas* ____

Competency 6
*Vocal descriptiveness, rate, vocal variety,
vocal energy* ____

Competency 7
*Conscious of vocal segregates
(um, uh, you know . . .) used only when needed* ____

Competency 8
Consistent point of view ____

Competency 9
Passion, ownership, knowledge of story ____

Competency 10
Eye contact (circle of awareness), face, postures, gestures ____

Competency 11
Preparation ____

Competency 12
Understanding/following the assignment ____

Remarks:

_____

FOLKTALE/FABLE:
Same point value

Competency 1
Effectiveness of prologue, title, author/unknown ____

Competency 2
Ownership, knowledge of story, cultural inferences ____

Competency 3
Consistent point of view, concentrated characters ____

Competency 4
Sequencing and possible rhythm, coherence ____

Competency 5
Variety of expression, mixture and use ____

Competency 6
Prepared for time constraint, editing ____

Competency 7
Sense of communication, audience engagement ____

Competency 8
Eye contact (circle of awareness), face, postures, gestures ____

Competency 9
Vocal filler (um, uh, etc. . . .) ____

Competency 10
Effective imagery conveyed ____

Competency 11
Preparation ____

Competency 12
Understanding/following the assignment ____

Final Remarks...

Even the most skilled storytellers don't subscribe to a single method for learning a story. Choose the methods best suited for you. Learn your story and anchor it with the powerful sense of purpose it contains. But do learn it. This means to own it. Feel it. Think it. You will do great!

"The invariable mark of wisdom is to see the miraculous in the ordinary."

—Ralph Waldo Emerson

Chapter 9
Working through Apprehension

Listen to ...

1. **"Nervous at First"**

   Guest Storyteller: Reverend Laura Mayo, July 3, 2014

   Listen to subtle signs of her apprehension and it suddenly went away. Why? She was having too much fun!

2. **"Joey"**

   Guest Storyteller: Larry Andrews, March 25, 2011

   Listen to this father whose need to tell the story about his autistic son, Joey, was more powerful than the apprehension he felt about delivering it. He told listeners at the beginning of his story that he wasn't really a storyteller. Really, Larry?

Understand

Causes of stage fright
Head, heart, gut
Poor platform behaviors
Mental imagery
Coaching
Feedback

*"Stage Fright? It's not the stage that scares me,
it's the audience."*

—Mark Twain

Stage Fright

The police who suspect him of killing his lover's husband want Jonathon Cooper, in Alfred Hitchcock's *Stage Fright*. Jonathon's friend and fellow acting student, Eve Gill, offers to hide him. However, he explains to Eve that the real killer was his lover, Charlotte Inwood. Eve decides to investigate herself, but when she meets the detective in charge of the case, she begins to fall in love. What a mess! Blackmail, manipulation, romance, and blistering intrigue are woven together in this vintage Hitchcock thriller. Trust me. The stage fright in this movie is far worse than the stage fright you will face when telling your story. Because in the film, stage fright is absolutely murder.

Nevertheless, do expect to have some stage fright. Even experienced storytellers admit to having some apprehension before telling a story. In fact, a degree of stage fright (synonymous with performance anxiety) can be motivating, actually adding a degree of excitement and anticipation for you, so long as the apprehension is not paralyzing to you. More specifically, if you were not the least bit nervous about telling a story to an audience, I might wonder if you really cared.

Stage fright is caused by the significant apprehension you feel about delivering your story. For most of us, symptoms of stage fright include butterflies, sweaty palms, dry throat, feeling faint, and imagining lapses in memory.

Stage fright can make you think that your listeners will find you boring, monotonous, or unprepared. It can make you worry that the room will be too warm or too cold; that you will trip over the microphone cord; that you will have a run in your stockings, your fly will be open, and some creepy crawling creature and his friends will be jogging on your face. Then we wonder what to do if any of those or other disaster fantasies occurs? We suddenly fear some impending doom or gloom—that some evil will be upon us. Please, save the analysis of foreboding for your literature professors, at least until you are able to control your stage fright. Alright, what now? Do we move around, look away from our listeners, cry, ask for forgiveness, or beg for extra credit? Do we leave the state?

Remember that stage fright is common for everyone, including your listeners. Therefore, do not fall prey to what researchers have known for years to be the primary culprit of stage fright: that we invest the others (listeners) with imagined power, especially in the ability to evaluate us and influence our eventual performance. Instead, let us meet stage fright head on.

What Do I Do?

Begin to field your stage fright by acknowledging that speech is a physiological process. In short, you need the right amount of energy to deliver your storytelling program comfortably. Even the most nervous teller can feel empowered when he is feeling energetic and in good spirits. Blending nervousness with energy creates nervous energy, the kind of anxiety that can inflate your desire to tell a tale rather than deflate your confidence by keeping the wind from your sail. So build your energy.

Exercise and eating right will go a long way to help keep your energy level in check, but learning to breathe correctly can prove to be the easiest and most amazing way to energize and keep stage fright somewhat out of sight. Before your rehearsals and just before you tell your story to your audience, relax and breathe deeply. Inhale. Exhale. Do it slowly. Deliberately. Privately. Close your eyes, and think about how well you know your story. Tell yourself that your story is more powerful than the anxiety you may feel about delivering it, and embrace mental imaging (see below). Realize how much you love your story and how much your listeners will love hearing it.

In the film *Walk the Line*, Johnny Cash is looking for work as a musician. He is unsuccessful until his soon-to-be producer says, "If you had to choose one song, Mr. Cash, one song you would sing if it was the last song you ever sang . . . the kind of song you'd sing while lying in the gutter, what song would it be?" Love your story as a singer loves a song. Believe it! Johnny Cash found work, and you will find your confidence. Love the idea about having the chance to communicate a story with a powerful message to people who need to hear it. Having a need to make your story known to other human beings is an overwhelming feeling and can offset even the worst case of performance anxiety.

Think about it. At what times in your life were you so compelled to thunder out your convictions that the only anxiety you felt was the anxiousness about making your point? What motivated you was your passion, steadfastness, devotion, and maybe love for the message you were so committed to tout. It is true that you probably won't be selecting a story with which you have a love affair for an assignment in class. But you might. And if not, you eventually will. Still, if you at least choose a story for an assignment you like a great deal, similar effects on reducing your stage fright can occur. Additionally, the more you care about your story the more you are able to solicit the responses you expect from your listeners. Therefore, if you have passion, you will probably have success.

Mental Imagery

Visualizing success is called mental imagery, and it is also a potentially powerful way to overcome paralyzing stage fright. Find a quiet place where you can be alone for awhile before telling your story. Ask yourself, "What will my audience see, feel, and touch as I tell my story?" "How will they respond to me when my storytelling proves effective?" Then, close your eyes and see your listeners laugh at your funny segments. Hear them. See them shed tears at sad moments. Watch them. See them leaning forward, anticipating your every word, waiting for an exciting climax, or cheering on the main character. See them wince, cringe, smile, and respond to you with the emotions you intended to access from them during your telling. Imagine getting the results you always wanted. And more.

Public speakers, athletes, even salespeople have successfully used mental imaging for many years. Like any other method for reducing performance anxiety, mental imaging does not promise that your storytelling experience will be free of anxiety and go exactly as planned, but those good things happen much more often than you think.

Head, Heart, Gut

Sometimes stage fright works like a wall, behind which people barricade themselves as if they are preparing to fend off an attack by their enemies. A nervous storyteller oftentimes perceives the audience to be the enemy, a group of people whose charge (no pun intended) is to ridicule and ultimately deface him. This is all imagined, of course. But latching on to the place in your body from where the story was first conceived can give a nervous teller the incentive—the key to unlocking the door and letting the audience in without fear of being dismissed as a person without something to say.

Unlocking that door can help you discover which body center, your head, heart, or gut, was the seed of your story. One of them serves as the origin of your story. Was it the well-thought force materializing in your head, the emotional force formed by your heart, or the instinctive raw force rising in your gut? This metaphorical discovery can help you stay tethered to the source of your story, and provide you with an uncanny sense of pride and conviction. Determining the body center from where your story comes is purely perceptual. Still, determining the body source of a story is a forceful, take-charge technique that can help you dissolve debilitating stage fright. It all starts with asking yourself, "From where did my story emerge?"

You told that fabulous story about what ignited your career change. That was a thoughtful and courageous decision, and it emanated from your head. Telling your high school sweetheart that you have always loved her was a beautifully tender and quixotic story, and it undoubtedly spawned from your heart. You mustered up enough courage to tell your father that you are fed up with him putting you down. You told him that he crushed you every time he humiliated you. You sounded strong when delivering that poignant story, and you commanded tremendous respect from your listeners. That story was born in your gut.

Asking yourself the "From where did the story come?" question also applies to stories that don't belong to you. The wisdom you conveyed through the folktale was an example of your extraordinary intelligence (from the head). You showed a sense of urgency when delivering the fable about the character's strength, fortitude, and unshakable determination (from the gut). The emphasis you placed on the queen's generosity was moving. It was clear from the story that you are charitable in every way (from the heart).

You are remarkable people, so learn how you became so brave, determined, tenacious, measured, forthright, and so much more. You will then be able to understand the force of that unplanned moment in your life, why that moment was strong enough to remain lodged in your memory, and so awesome that you constructed it into a momentous story. Now you have the edge you need to get up there and tell your story.

The most effective thing about this technique as a way to work through your stage fright is that only you can decide on head, heart, or gut as the birthplace of your story. Unlock the door and speak from your head, heart, or gut. You may find yourself digging from all three. Your story is powerful. Let your listeners in.

Poor Platform Behaviors

There was a speech professor in college who referred to the front of the room as the platform. He called it a platform because he didn't think it sounded as threatening as a stage. Fine. Let's just say that many students in his class had "platform fright." Actually, I liked the word. Nevertheless, whether you call it a platform or stage, it represents the location from where the teller will tell. Over the years, I observed how perfectly confident and prepared students would turn into nervous wrecks as soon as they left their seats to walk up to the front of the room. For years, it was all I could do to keep from looking at these students and shout, "Dead Man Walking," because they looked like they were headed to their execution.

Then I tried something in one of my storytelling classes a few semesters ago. In a practice round on telling personal narratives, I asked students to begin telling their narratives from their seats. After a few moments, I prompted them to stand and continue telling their stories while walking up to the platform. They would finish their stories after positioning themselves on the platform, facing their listeners. There were virtually no signs of stage fright exhibited by the students when they reached the front of the classroom. As the results would suggest, students found this technique very helpful in reducing stage fright. The reason for this is not very profound. They found the stage to be a stark reminder that they will be in the spotlight, along with all of the uncomfortable behaviors that come with it.

Starting a presentation from your seat can create a less formal impression and reduce the anxiety that traditionally accompanies a more formal one. Not every presentation can begin from your seats. However, conducting this "seat-to-stage" exercise for a few practice rounds could be just the ticket in helping you to reduce troubling stage fright. So, you find yourself up there and anxiety hits you anyway? Relax. You want to put yourself in a position to regain focus on your story, and be calm enough to draw on the variety of expression you need to tell the story well. As you reclaim that focus, don't do things that will exasperate your anxiety. Staying away from these performance no-no's will help you to take control over those anxious moments:

Do not move too much. Unmotivated pacing does little to calm the nerves but can do quite a bit to rattle an audience. Appropriate movement consists of gestures and postures designed to enhance a story, and not a set of meaningless moves intended to relieve personal tension. Put yourself in a secure stance when delivering your story. Plant your feet on the ground, but don't place them too parallel to each other. Place your right foot slightly higher than your left foot. Don't do the hokey pokey and turn yourself around because that's not what it's all about. It's about keeping your legs from shaking like a palm tree on the eve of a hurricane.

Don't be a fidgeter. Fidgeters tend to play with things while telling their stories—stuff that detracts from the storytelling experience. For example, leave your pens at your desk (you won't be doing any writing up there anyway). I remember a student who once brought his pen to the front of the room and played with it while telling his story. The pen leaked all over him. Somehow, he managed to finish his story but no one could have told you what his story was about. Stop playing with your hair, buttons, collar, and eyeglasses. None of these items are story props. Jinglers are those who find it necessary to place their hands in their pockets and jingle change, keys, and other metal objects housed in their pockets. "Hmmm, how much change does he have?" is not a question we should be pondering while you tell your story. Keep your hands out of your pockets. That's that!

If you forget to use vocal variety when telling your story, you run a high risk of becoming a tranquilizer—someone sounding like verbal valium, lulling listeners to sleep with a palpable monotonous tone. And please don't be a mumbler. Mumbling isn't just for the anxious anymore. Even the boldest among us will mumble if we do not use our mouths. Your mouth is a muscle. Stretch it when you speak but don't go overboard, or you will sound ridiculous. Just don't sound like you're hung over or have marbles in your mouth. Articulate and enunciate clearly, and you will purr like a pro.

Practice, Practice, Practice

When I was a kid, I wanted to play guitar like Neil Diamond (yes, he is alive and still singing). After my obnoxious ranting and raving, my mother bought me a guitar. She signed me up for weekly lessons. Each week I pretended to know what I was doing. I didn't have a clue. And there was good reason: I never practiced. I told my instructor that I practiced, but he knew better. He was on to me.

Why wouldn't he be? Each week I played the same stupid chord and continuously asked him how to use the guitar pick. It might as well have been a harmonica.

Practice doesn't make perfect, but it does keep you from looking like a fool, not to mention how not practicing fuels stage fright. Award-winning storyteller Doug Lipman points out that "practicing" in our culture connotes doing something alone. This connotation does not really apply to practicing your story. This is not to say that practicing alone cannot be helpful. Sometimes a storyteller needs to lock himself away and present his stories to an imaginary audience and be free of concern for the reactions of others. But practicing alone too much or too long can produce some unfortunate results. It may result in an inflexible version of your story; you may become too focused on choosing exact words and ways to say them; you may become less sensitive to communicating the story and more inclined to recite it; and you will not be accustomed to the variety of feedback given by an attentive audience.

Face it; you need to practice your stories in front of others. Others? Aren't they the reason I suffer from performance anxiety in the first place? Strangers are the culprits of your angst, so find a few friends who are willing to spend some time listening to you. Trust in your friends, and let your story develop through informal telling with them. And don't think that performing your story is the only practice option. You can simply relate a personal experience with friends and solicit their advice on how to make your story grow. What did they find funny? What made them smile? What part of the experience made them think? Likewise, you can tell your friends about a story you are reading or a folktale you want to revisit. Talking about these stories with friends can be as useful as telling a story to them.

You have no friends? Search for supportive groups whose mission is to listen to tellers like you. Look for storyteller guilds in your city, continuing education workshops on storytelling or reducing stage fright, and local festivals where you can practice your storytelling skills. Membership in one of the many storytelling associations, especially the *National Storytelling Network*, can serve as a terrific contact where you get some useful tips about storytelling from a range of tellers, and have an opportunity to exchange ideas about any and every aspect of storytelling. Also take advantage of moments when you can tell a story as part of your conversation or short speech, such as at a family gathering, a meeting with your civic association, or that toast to your special friend. Oh, I forgot. You have no friends.

Be a Coach, Not Critic

Alright, you heard enough about stage fright, but I would like to offer one final quick-hitter: say mean things to a storyteller about his performance and rest assured you will propel him into a whole new kingdom of fear. And he won't be telling another story for a very long time . . . thanks to you. Learn to promote confidence in others by furnishing feedback that will induce rather than reduce the teller's anxiety. Besides, providing meaningful feedback to your fellow tellers is an ideal way to display the manner in which you want to receive feedback in kind. You would also be making a strong statement about supporting those who wish to improve their storytelling skills. Learning a story is important, but learning ways to deliver meaningful and supportive feedback is more about learning to be a storyteller. That's a valuable lesson.

Meaningful feedback is certainly honest feedback, but it would be easy to take the concept of honesty too far. A teller asks, "What did you think of my storytelling?" and you thoughtfully answer, "I thought it sucked more than anything I have heard given by any mammal at any time in my life." Thoughtful? Are you kidding me? Spilling your criticism with the same frankness as Don Rickles (stop saying, "Huh?" and look him up on YouTube) on his greatest night of performance is not thoughtful feedback. Don Rickles is paid well to insult people. You get nothing from your abrasive spatter other than the unfortunate experience of annihilating someone's self-image.

For feedback to be truly constructive, it must be communicated in a way so that the criticism is clear, helpful, and kind. To be truly critical is to offer feedback that can help the listener to modify his behavior for the better. Therefore, we need to learn how to issue feedback that is both honest and listenable to tellers, not the destructive sort that comes from a mind that works like a gumball machine, swiftly dropping harmful dribble from our brains to our tongues effortlessly.

To begin, storyteller and education coach Kevin Cordi recommends that we adopt the role of "coach" instead of critic. A coach connotes the helpful mentor and someone who brings a constant splash of support in every piece of feedback he delivers, even the kind that initially smacks of rejection. A coach is concerned about helping the teller improve and feel encouraged. When you imagine yourself as coach rather than critic, you listen attentively and involve the teller in the feedback process.

When taking on the role of coach, it is important to keep in mind that not all tellers may want feedback, at least until they learn to trust your comments and insights. Therefore, it is always best to ask the teller if he desires feedback. If the answer is "No," then move on, while refraining from any ridiculing or sarcastic response. When the teller is ready for feedback, make sure he feels he is contributing to the process and that his feelings are respected.

If a teller requests feedback, always start by telling him what you liked about his story. If you cannot find anything you like, then train yourself to find something you enjoyed, and be sure that what you find is not manufactured. Make your comment real. Making up some positive remark serves no one. Keep in mind that people enjoy telling stories and most of them want to improve, so openly applaud the teller's desire to confront the challenges of storytelling. It is also a good idea to praise first, and then offer suggestions when giving feedback.

When you begin your feedback with explicit suggestions, the teller may not hear you praise the positive aspects of his telling. The teller is a real person with feelings, and your feedback must consider the teller before the story. When praise is given, be specific. Saying, "Good Job" does not help the teller improve. If you receive an "A" on an assignment, would you not want specific feedback about your great efforts so you can do it again? The same holds true with praising the efforts of the storyteller. For example, learn to substitute comments like "I loved your voice" with "I enjoyed the way you used your voice to make the frog come to life."

Your goal might be to offer feedback that can help the teller perform a particular story better, but the teller may be telling the story to pay tribute to his mother or for a special occasion. Listen carefully to the teller's goals for telling his story, and help him guide the story in the right direction. Through your feedback, encourage tellers to try new voices, experiment with new beginnings and endings, or to stretch the boundaries of imagination in a number of ways. In short, help the storyteller take risks by offering words of encouragement to accompany your words of wisdom.

Review a teller's progress by giving immediate, rather than delayed feedback. Point out the measurable improvements made by the teller, as well as the level of confidence and poise you see him gaining each time he tells a tale. Be certain that the feedback you give infuses the storyteller with an upward spiral of success. The idea behind coach rather than critic is that we want feedback to push a storyteller forward without the fear that comes with harsh review.

We must reward the teller for his efforts, not condemn him for mistakes. Feedback, although explicit and candid, should allow the teller to feel safe, respected, and skilled. If your feedback does not do this, it might be best to offer very little criticism or none at all until you are able to render comments with the similar skill and preparation you expect from the performance you plan to critique.

Looking in All the Wrong Places?

If you are not enrolled in a storytelling course and need to solicit some feedback for your upcoming telling, there is a good chance you will be scrambling to search for the feedback you need. So look for places where you can tell. Toastmasters International is the consummate organization for those interested in harnessing their fundamental speaking skills, as well as an opportunity to listen and observe how feedback is given.

Also, volunteer to tell stories at schools, libraries, and community festivals. As a way to practice your craft constantly while yielding substantial feedback along the way, learn to put together theme-based story programs for special occasions, and offer to tell the stories at those occasions. Take those three birthday stories to your little sister's tenth birthday party, and tell them to her friends. Then, ask them what they thought (if you dare). Most importantly, be sure to network with other storytellers at local and national storytelling associations to find opportunities for telling as many stories as you can. I give you a list of possible networks at the end of this text.

Final Remarks...

Feeling anxious about telling a story in front of an audience is to be expected. Sources of apprehension can usually be identified and controlled. Although apprehension never completely disappears, it is ultimately your desire to tell your story that should overshadow any fears you have about delivering it. In short, let your passion relieve the tension in your body and mind. Be kind when giving feedback to fellow tellers. Ask them for ideas. Thank them for their time. There is a great chance they will thank you for your story.

"Another world is not only possible,
she is on her way.
And on a quiet day, if you really listen,
you can hear her breathing."

—Arundhati Roy

Chapter 10

I Heard It through the Radio

Listen to ...

1. **"Now this Works!"**

   Guest Storyteller: Maxine Lennon, June 3, 2013

   Listen to a show that spotlights one of the best radio tellers around. She is also a voice-over talent, which comes in handy at times. Listen from beginning to end and contemplate timing, rhythm, banter, responses, movement, and theme.

2. **"The Child in All of Us?"**

   Guest Storyteller: Sheila Starks Phillips, Jo Rader, and Jo Harper, April 10, 2009

   Listen to a show that spotlights some heavy-hitters in children's storytelling. These tellers are also authors and offer insights about the difference in oral versus written telling. Be ready to revisit your childhood . . . and not wanting to return.

Understand

Imagination
Radio preparation
Radio as an extension of you
Current implications of radio telling
Guided scripts

"Understanding is nothing else than conception caused by speech."

—*Thomas Hobbes*

Imagine That!

Few educational benefits of storytelling are more vital than imagination. Imagination enables us to see it all by allowing us to tap into all the infinite possibilities of the universe. By imagining, we form mental images, sensations, and concepts when they are not perceived through sight, hearing, or other senses. Imagination expressed through stories was created from the inspiration of someone's imagination, and the radio has long encouraged imagination of unfathomable proportion for teller and listener alike. With no visual component, storytelling and human drama told on the radio depend on dialogue, music, and sound effects to paint story pictures, complete with a clear plot, sense of time, and characters with which listeners can establish a relationship.

The decades of the 1930s and 1940s were times when radio drama (the most popular context of radio telling), was the leading form of entertainment. If you ever doubt how imagination is successfully triggered by radio drama, consider "The War of the Worlds," an adaptation of H. G. Wells' novel aired on CBS on October 30, 1938. Directed and narrated by Orson Welles, the first two-thirds of the sixty-minute broadcast was told as if it was a series of news bulletins. Welles was so brilliant in his storytelling that millions of listeners were convinced that Martians had invaded the country.

"The War of the Worlds" was radio drama incarnate, and Welles was the iconic radio storyteller. Throughout the middle of the twentieth century, masses of avid listeners tuned in to enjoy a variety of dramatic productions, soap operas, comedies, and musical theater. Americans even cozily huddled in front of the family radio to listen to the resolve in President Franklin Roosevelt's rhetoric during his popular fireside chats. Even on the radio, listeners cited the image of a cardigan-clad President seated in front of a crackling fire that guided them into an air of calm, amidst a world of turbulence and mayhem.

Today, radio drama has minimal presence—restricted mostly to podcasts of programs from previous decades. But if you listen to Garrison Keillor and other great tellers (www.talkzone.com), you know that telling stories for the purpose of entertainment is hardly dead. In addition, entertaining stories told on the radio for the purpose to tell and sell have become common. Often I have tuned in just in time to hear the broker tell the story about the family who survived a financial crisis, thanks to his skills. Then there is the physician who tells the story about a patient who came back from a near-death experience. The mayor divulges how he recaptured the lost trust of an entire city, and the lawyer recounts the story about the way his client was mistreated by police. These examples represent hundreds of such stories heard daily on the radio, because storytelling on the radio has become a widespread and popular art form for communicating essential information about health, education, international business, religion, and more. Also, any successful radio talk show in the current market has its share of storytellers whose autobiographic monologues, oral histories, folkloric stories, and social commentaries are standard program features.

Storytelling on the radio may have a different format than in past years, but it is still an indispensable art form for modern radio. So in case you are asked to tell a story on the air (you're thinking, "Fat chance!"), let us talk about some important ways to handle it.

Getting Cozy on the Air

As sung by **The Buggles** in the first video ever shown on MTV on August 1, 1981, video may have killed the radio star, but radio did not kill the storyteller. In fact, the radio is a refreshing venue for the teller, because it helps him establish a unique kind of intimacy with his listeners. It is unique because the intimacy is established with listeners who come together by tuning in, not by forming a physical gathering. In other words, most members of the listening audience are listening alone. We are in our cars on the way to work, sitting at our desks, preparing a meal, reading at home, before going to sleep, and the like. Just you and the radio guy. That's intimate.

Interestingly, a successful radio teller tries to create that sense of closeness with his listeners the same way a storyteller tries to create it on the physical stage. The difference is that the teller on the air needs to imagine that he is the one alone, as he harnesses his skills and uses them to tell stories to a very real, but unseen, set of listeners who occupy the space that surrounds him. In short, the radio need not be a physical barrier to a teller if the teller sees it as an extension of himself.

Effective radio tellers try hard to communicate on the air the way they communicate face-to-face. They know that their ability to sustain the same, or at least similar, communication style on the radio as they do in person stands them in good stead with their listeners, because it is a way to build trust with their listeners. Trust is an established pattern of consistency where the verbal and nonverbal messages conveyed by the person can be relied upon. We do not trust inconsistent people.

It might be helpful to consider the similarity between establishing trust on the radio to the way it is established on the telephone. I don't want any of you to revisit recent nightmares, but just for a moment think about the less than stellar customer service representative you called about a problem with your recent statement. True, there are good customer service representatives, but you and I don't get them. We get the ones who aren't just having a bad day; they're having a bad life. And it's our fault! Do you ever wonder if the miserable human being on the other end of the line would be that miserable if the phone was not there to protect him?

The telephone is an extension of you. If you are miserable on the phone, the listener will more than likely peg you as a miserable person. Period. Therefore, it is best to communicate on the phone as if the phone wasn't there. You will want to smile when you speak, watch your tone, try not to interrupt, and for goodness sakes don't keep anyone on hold longer than it takes to breathe deeply for seven seconds (personal suggestion). Those tips for talking on the phone also apply if you take calls on the air. Like the telephone, the radio is a physical extension of the storyteller; and, like the phone, it is best to tell stories to listeners as if the radio was not there.

Okay. You are waiting for your radio telling time. You get the cue: "You're on the air." And you panic? Stop that. Just follow these suggestions: Close your eyes before hearing the words to your story. Go ahead. The audience can't see you. Get yourself comfortable. See the story in front of you. Set the scene in your mind. Make sure you wear your headset so you are able to hear what you sound like. Monitor your pace. Force yourself to slow down. Intensify the action in your story by vocally emphasizing the critical elements in your story. Get your listeners to know the characters in your story. Have fun with their personalities, and be sure that those tuning in can depict the two characters in the dialogues you recreate.

Besides the gestures of your host, fellow guests, or the engineer, there will not be anyone in front of you giving you feedback. Therefore, it is essential that you monitor yourself. Do you find yourself gesturing while telling your story? Great. Keep it up. It means you're into your story. Those gestures, postures, and the like are great ways to imagine that your audience is in the studio.

Concentrate and focus on your task relentlessly. Radio formats and time restrictions can be maddening, so don't deviate from the story you prepared. Because radio programs have defined limits, be sure you craft a story to fit within those limits and plan a few extra seconds of space in case you need to recover from any problems. Also, be sure to include enough time for providing your Web page and general announcements or personal information relevant to the program in which you told your story. For example, where will you be performing Friday night (standing room only, of course)? Are you a member of an organization you want to advertise? When does your club meet? Will you be part of an ongoing series on the radio program? Are there any phone numbers, addresses, or directions you need to give your listeners?

Banter (light chat) is sometimes included on talk radio (where most storytelling is told). If the host engages you in banter before your story, be brief, clear with responses, and thank your host. If banter begins after you tell your story, feel great about what you have just accomplished, and carry that feeling with you when answering questions.

Listen to the selection of KPFT programs designated in this chapter and the stories assigned in other chapters, each found on your online supplement to this text. A full list of programs can be found on www.houstonstorytellers.org. Go to "Radio Program" on the menu in the left margin, click, and enjoy. Listen to ways in which stories, themes, banter, music, introductions, and mandatory station breaks blend to create a defined occasion for listeners. Also take notice of the research I conducted about each teller and the show's theme to create a heightened level of comfort for the guest teller. Comfort is an essential prerequisite for establishing the kind of intimacy needed between teller, host, and audience. To better illustrate these features I have included a few scripts from previous shows in the appendix for your consideration. Take note of the idiosyncratic details, because the best way to create a naturally flowing feeling on a show that features storytellers is to be ridiculously prepared.

Final Remarks...

The first electronic medium of mass entertainment, radio continues to engage and influence listeners through its deceptively intimate characteristics. Consequently, due to the special connection between air-time tellers and the listener, radio remains a highly sought-after venue for many storytellers.

> *"Always say time changes things,*
> *but you actually have to change them yourself."*
>
> *—Andy Warhol*

Epilogue

My favorite reason for telling stories is that the story becomes a talking window, an instrument I use to determine how my listeners should enter into my life. Depending on the story and the way that I tell it, my listeners may come through that window with caution, skepticism, or anticipation. Listeners sometimes come through the window with wonder or trepidation. I have watched them enter with disbelief, disgust, and even a little distrust. Some enter with hopes of somehow seeing themselves in the stories I tell about human attributes and foibles. They peek inside the window to search for tantalizing clues of optimism and hope, and above all, love.

I want my listeners to return to my windows, because when I open them, human hearts and minds become connected. Through this connection, each of us becomes a part of something greater than we can achieve alone. It cannot possibly get any better than that. For me, these moving words by John Steinbeck speak to the very core of the relationship between storytelling and human connection:

"We are all lonesome animals. We spend all our life trying to be less lonesome. One of our ancient methods is to tell a story begging the listener to say, and to feel, 'Yes, that is the way it is, or at least that is the way I feel it.' You're not as alone as you thought."

As I see it, people who keep others from coming through their windows are keeping great gifts from those who want to visit, and even greater gifts from themselves. There was a story…

…about a farmer who had so many beautiful crops, he would set traps for all the animals whom he feared would destroy them. The birds and the squirrels and raccoons never came. The farmer thought himself successful until one day he realized how terribly

lonely he was. So, he walked out to the middle of his field and held out his arms to welcome the animals. Not one creature came, for they all feared the farmer's new scarecrow.

Let down your arms and let others in through the power of your stories.

Appendix A

Sample Radio Scripts

Script 1

Music Intro: about 45 seconds before fade down

Cue Down/Signal Mike

10:00:

An unknown poet once wrote: "The leaves are green, the nuts are brown, they hang so high and won't come down. Leave them alone till frosty weather, when they will all fall down cozily together." That may be my rhythmic wish for a cold front, but luckily, I'd like to think, you've tuned into something very cool: *So, What's Your Story,* the place to help kick-start your weekend…every weekend, on listener-sponsored KPFT 90.1. FM Houston. I am your host, Dr. Hank Roubicek, Professor of Communication at the University of Houston Downtown.

Thanks for joining me, and if this is your first listen, this is what we do: *So, What's Your Story* spotlights soul-inspired tellers, both starters and stars, who engage us with absorbing personal stories and treasured folktales by taking us on enchanted journeys and then, returning us safely to the present. We've gone from monthly to weekly to prime, thanks to you, because it is your support that keeps KPFT tuned into your life. Tonight is the last night of our fall fund drive at KPFT, and I'm asking you to help us end strong. We need about $300.00 to reach our goal and have 30 minutes to do it. Please call our pride-fueled volunteers at pledge central with your donations at 713-526-5738 (KPFT) to let us know you want us around. Corporate-free, expression-rich programs frame our unique, eclectic inventory here at KPFT, and you won't hear any of it anywhere else.

Programmers receive No pay. We do it for Love, and anything you can afford will go farther than you can ever fathom. $35.00 will buy you a KPFT membership, support your favorite show by donating some of your monthly coffee money, and know that whatever you can give will keep KPFT workin' for you as the only listener-sponsored, open and free broadcast venue in Houston. You know, when Pacifica was born in the 1940s, many doubted the viability of a broadcast model which didn't rely on corporate funding or government intervention. But the need for open expression—for thoughts and ideas to be rendered freely superseded any need to be regulated by business. That's our mission here at KPFT, because we're all about you. This is your station. And we need your help.

I'm always amazed by the number of story-lover listeners in Houston and surrounding areas, and that was punctuated by the astounding 600% donated over my goal during the short August drive and tonight, thanks to their online donations, I want to thank Toni, Martha, Robert, and Karen for their generous hearts. You too can donate online if **A**, you don't like phones or **B** if 10:00 is past your bedtime. Just go to kpft.org, then donations, and scroll to *So, What's Your Story* to keep us in your lives every Thursday night at 10.

10:05:

When you call 713-526-5738, you'll be able to claim some cool thank you gifts, each a must–have for every story lover. **Roxie:** (Read gifts), **Roxie Continue**: Then: Call in your donations and tell us what you want.

10:08:

We are all about community, but no one holds a candle to the courageous, talented, and compassionate special guest joining me tonight. Jillian J.J. Simmons, daytime host on Houston's KBXX, 97.9 FM, "The Box," J.J.'s captivated listeners in her hometown of Cincinnati, Dayton, New York City's WBLS, and has interviewed a plethora of important people including a man by the name of Barack Obama. Dedicated to empowering others, she gave birth to the *I'm Me Foundation*, as well as a beautiful daughter who is fortunate enough to know what it means to build character, thanks to her Mom. Perhaps most important, J.J.'s book, "Without Bruises," is a testament to her unwavering need to guide others by chronicling her experiences from an abusive relationship and the best way to stress the significance of Domestic Violence Awareness Month, going on right now. J.J., I am so glad you are here.

J.J., your story is about healing, courage, and hope. Before you share your story, tell us about Domestic Violence Awareness month (Respond in 30 seconds max.).

10:10:

Your story tonight is designed to provide us with a clear understanding of your book. Tell us your story (6–7 minutes max.).

10:17:

Host: Comment. You are listening to guest teller, J.J. Simmons of 97.9 The Box on *So, What's Your Story?* This is Hank Roubicek and Roxy Russell.

So, What's Your Story, is about validating lives through story; it's about the power of narrative, and we need your support by calling 713-526-5738 (KPFT), so we can continue to bring you the best in storytelling. J.J.'s story represents the power of poignancy, not unlike the story about his mother's last Christmas, or the vision about his sister's death, that first kiss with Dad watching through the window; folktales about the Bookbinder—waiting to document the story of your life as you pass into the other world, that mean fairy, wicked babysitter, slow-movin' rabbit, and the bagpipe that didn't like the way she looked in plaid love letters, diaries, stories which yield tears and smiles and laughter and awe every week, and we need you to keep it all in check by calling 713-526-5738 (KPFT) or by getting online to kpft.org, then scrolling to *So, What's Your Story?* And listen, I know every amount is a lot so don't worry about paying it all at once. (I'll send Roxy to your home to craft a payment plan.) You can always stop by the station at 419 Lovett, grab a bagel and I'll even tell you a story. Roxy, please remind us of those impeccable thank you gifts. **Roxy:** Read list of gifts (abbreviated version, 30 seconds max.).

10:20:

The theme of empowerment will continue next week as guest, Businesswoman, Laura Nelson, will share stories about overcoming obstacles right here on KPFT 90.1 FM. We are ending our fund drive in just a few minutes—and needing your help, by calling 713-526-5738 and telling us we matter… that you care about a station committed to bringing you a collection of programs found only on Pacific. Then, a great Halloween show with Texas teller, Brian Herod, followed by students from Johnston Middle School, moving into family stories and, in December, we'll introduce a call-in version so I can ask you "So, What's Your Story?"

10:21:

J.J., tell us about your "Without Bruises: Help, Hope, and Heal Series" going on between now and January 2014. How can we learn more? (Respond in about 30–45 seconds max.).

10:22:

Thanks, J.J. *Reiterate Cause.* Imagine tuning into KPFT and hearing this: **Silence.** Nothing. Your donations keep everything running from transmitters to equipment to programs, all resulting in listener-sponsored, free-speech anchored, Houston-only KPFT so please let us know that you want storytelling to be a standard on Houston radio by calling pledge central at 713-526-5738. This is Hank Roubicek and Roxy Russell with special guest, J.J. Simmons from 97.9.

10:23:

Telling stories is a big part of this program, but so is Tip for the Teller, a segment that will be continued in two weeks. Roxy, please tell us what this is and how listeners can reach us with questions and possible guest spots: Hank, Tip for the Teller is when we learn something about storytelling from a question asked by one of our listeners. We respond to one every week. If listeners have questions they'd like us to answer on the air or want to be a guest on *So, What's Your Story,* send questions or story ideas to (be sure to spell roubey) roubey.story@gmail.com (repeat). We will get back to you.

Thank You, Roxy. Another tip: Every story lover belongs in the Houston Storytellers Guild. We hold a monthly Story Swap on the third Tuesday of every month, from 7–8:30 PM, at St. Andrews House, 1811 Heights Blvd. It's a group that rocks! Check out our site at www.houstonstorytellers.org for all the fun happenings.

Just a short few moments left to call in your pledge at 713-526-5738 (KPFT) or go online to kpft.org and help us stay alive and kickin'.

10:27:55: (Regardless of where I am): Start music low

Thank you, J.J. Simmons, day host with 97.9FM, The Box, for your mettle and inspiration. This is Hank Roubicek on *So, What's Your Story,* one of the power hour programs on this Thursday night on KPFT 90.1 Houston. Scooter is next with the Inner Side. Make KPFT a part of every day and make it a habit to tune in every Thursday at 10:00 PM for *So, What's Your Story,* and ease into the weekend right. Be good to each other. I'm Dr. Hank Roubicek always reminding you it's Never Too Late to Live Happily Ever After.

10:29:

When I am finished, raise volume on music and play until 10:29.

Engineer's Note: 10:28:

Wherever I am, start music softly to cue me a few seconds before 10:27:55. I will shoot for completion by no later than 10:28:30. Raise volume when I'm done and let music roll until 10:29.

Script 2

Music Intro: about 45 seconds before fade down

Cue Down/Signal Mike

10:00:

'Tis the season for a lot of things; not the least of which is rediscovering our family by telling stories about them, from life-changing events to troubling introspections. Stories help us reconcile or revive a connection of some kind. Family means no one gets lost or forgotten…that's the message dispatched when family tales are told…tonight's warming thought on *So, What's Your Story* on KPFT 90.1 FM, the coolest place on your dial, because we spotlight extraordinary tellers, both starters and stars, who share at least one thing in common: Each is an extraordinary person, who engages us with stirring personal stories and treasured folktales by taking us on enchanted journeys and then, returning us safely to the present… and a show that can be enjoyed only on listener-sponsored KPFT Houston. I am your host, Dr. Hank Roubicek, Professor of Communication at the University of Houston Downtown.

Tonight is a prelude to our call-in shows the next two Thursdays, December 19 and 26, when you share your 2–3 minute holiday stories, many of which will undoubtedly be anchored around our families. Few tellers can demonstrate the power that embodies a family narrative better than my guest, Jay Stailey. Jay's been a frequent guest on this show because he personifies the soul of the consummate teller: candid, engaging, poignant. Jay's range represents his capacity to reach every kind of listener and student with his signature intimate style, a style defined by Katie Galloway, my guest from a couple of weeks ago…the young woman who mesmerized us with her story about House of Pies, complete with the emotional turbulence with which it was carved. She is a product of Professor Stailey's Storytelling course at UHD, and I am hoping to ambush more of his students to become guest tellers in upcoming weeks.

Jay just returned from his stint as featured teller at the Sneem Ireland Storytelling and Folklore festival. His book, *Short Tales Tall Tales and Tales of Medium Stature* will be released as an e-book by Parkhurst Brothers Publishing in April 2014. He is two-time winner of the Greater Houston Area's Liar's Contest, was three times a featured teller at the George West Storyfest, and a teller-in-residence at the International Storytelling Center in Jonesborough, Tennessee…and that's a very short list of his achievements. A member of the Houston Storyteller's Guild, colleague, friend, and a real sport for being here because like most old people, it's past his bedtime.

10:05:

Hi, Jay. Last time it was Monday at 6:00 AM, now 10:00 at night. Let's talk about Katie for a moment. She was outstanding. If her stories didn't touch you, then we need to check our pulse. (I will take a moment to remind listeners about the story). **To Jay:** What do we discover about ourselves from disclosing these stories? What is uncovered? (Respond in 30 seconds max.).

10:06:

Jay, you have a story about each your Mom and Dad. What's your first story?

Jay's First Story: (4–6 minutes max.).

10:12:

Host: Comment. This is Hank Roubicek with Roxy Russell, from whom you'll hear in a moment, and you are listening to guest storyteller, Jay Stailey on *So, What's Your Story?* On KPFT 90.1 FM Houston, 89.5 in Galveston, and 90.3 in Livingston. **To Roxy:** Do you have a favorite holiday family flick? (Respond in a few seconds). **To Jay:** What about you? Favorite family-holiday movie come to mind? (Respond in a few seconds). Host may mention one here…**To Roxy:** Roxy, let's tell our listeners about the call-in shows for the next two weeks. **Roxy:** Hank, we are asking for memories frozen in time and ready to thaw. Prepare a 2–3 minute holiday story and tell it on the air by calling 713-526-5738 during the show. Memorable holidays with family, friends, or alone? Arguments, meaningful gifts, in-laws, travel, birth, loss, revelations. Be sure to keep it under 3 minutes. Be sure to join us on Facebook, *So, What's Your Story?* for more ideas and **Like** us when you leave.

10:13:

Host: Thanks, Roxy. Reflect on Jay's stories in the past (in those categories). **To Jay:** Suggestions for listeners about preparing their stories? (Respond in 30 seconds max.). **Host:** Something I see time and time again is that people are pretty forgiving when it comes to other's family. The only family that horrifies us is our own. Cary Grant said, "Insanity runs in my family. It practically gallops." OK, let's get back to the person who is truly entertaining. Jay, tell us about your next story (Respond in a few seconds). Then, what's your story?

10:15:

Jay's Second Story: (4–6 minutes max.)

10:21:

Host: Comment. This is Hank Roubicek with Roxy Russell. You are listening to *So, What's Your Story?* On KPFT 90.1 Houston, with Jay Stailey, ushering in the holiday season with stories about family

10:22:

Host: Comment. Roxy, it's time for Tip for the Teller, a segment when we learn something about storytelling from a question asked by one of our listeners. What's tonight's question? **Roxy:** Mark from Houston wants to know, "Dr. Hank, do you have suggestions about movies about Storytelling?" Hey, Mark. I think someone else asked this at one time and I love answering it. I loved both *Finding Neverland* with Johnnie Depp and *Big Fish* starring Albert Finney. Depp plays Scottish playwright, James Barrie, who cultivates a relationship with a family who inspired him to write *Peter Pan*. It's a beautiful, poignant story about the evolution of crafting a story, and the revelation that adults who imagine don't grow up. Reconciliation between a dying father and his son is the central theme in *Big Fish*. Edward's son, Will, pulls together themes and characters from his father's storied life—a life first viewed as collective fakery, to learn that his father is a man of great substance. There is little fantastic about Edward Bloom and, in the end, it is his fantastic stories that bring them closer together. Two very cool movies I recommend for anyone interested in learning more about the power of story. Hope that helps, Mark. And thanks for asking. If you have a question you want answered or want to be a guest on *So, What's Your Story*, Roxy will tell you how to make it happen.

10:24:

Roxy: We love questions and story ideas, so send as many as you like to (be sure to spell roubey) roubey.story@gmail.com (repeat). We will get back to you. Don't you dare forget our call-in shows the next two weeks; December 19th and 26th, when we'll listen to your 2–3 minute holiday stories. Call 713-526-5738 and we'll listen to as many as we can. Join us on Facebook, on *So, What's Your Story*, so we can remind you of the number to call. And while you're thinking about the story you'll tell when you call, think about getting to the monthly story swap held by the Houston Storytellers Guild on the third Tuesday of every month, from 7–8:30 PM, at St. Andrews House, 1811 Heights Blvd. And check out our site at www.houstonstorytellers.org for all the fun happenings.

Host: Thank You, Roxy. **Host:** Possible Family Joke here…

Jay, researchers have long postulated that teenagers who listen to their family stories tend to develop a strong intergenerational self. **To Jay:** What are your thoughts? (Respond in about 30 seconds max.). **Host:** Thoughts about my son not knowing what I learned.

10:26:

Host: I'm convinced that sharing and listening to stories about our families can help us become healthier emotional beings. We learn about our seeds, our nuclei, our destinies. We are reminded we are a part of something. Jay Stailey, thank you for being a part of our lives this evening. It is always an honor and a pleasure to have you in the studio and I look forward to your students joining me soon.

10:27:55:

(Regardless of where I am): Start music low

To all our listeners, keep loving a great story and I'll keep bringing them to you. Call us next week. This is Hank Roubicek and Roxy Russell on *So, What's Your Story,* one of the power hour programs on this Thursday night on KPFT 90.1 FM Houston. Make KPFT a part of everyday and make it a habit to tune in every Thursday at 10:00 PM and ease into the weekend right. Don't move, because Scooter is next with the *Inner Side.* Be good to each other. I'm Dr. Hank Roubicek always reminding you it's Never Too Late to Live Happily Ever After.

10:29:

When I am finished, raise volume on music and play until 10:29.

Engineer's Note: 10:28:

Wherever I am, start music softly to cue me a few seconds before 10:27:55. I will shoot for completion by no later than 10:28:30. Raise volume when I'm done and let music roll until 10:29.

Script 3

Music Intro: about 45 seconds before fade down

Cue Down/Signal Mike

10:00:

Robert Browning wrote, "Days decrease And Autumn grows, autumn is everything." Fall is here, it's Thursday night, and you've tuned into *So, What's Your Story,* the coolest place to help kick-start your weekend on listener-sponsored KPFT 90.1. I am your host,

Dr. Hank Roubicek, Professor of Communication at the University of Houston Downtown.

STATEMENTS ABOUT PAST SHOWS: monthly to weekly to prime, thanks to you, So, What's Your Story spotlights soul-inspired tellers, both pros and newbies, who engage us with revealing personal stories and beloved folktales by taking us—alluring us, on enchanted journeys and then, returning us safely to the present.

10:03:

Aloha, Rebecca. Most don't know the complete meaning of the word. *Question:* "Tell us." (Respond in about 30 seconds max.). Host: I'm amazed by how deities in Hawaiian mythology are similar to those in Greek mythology: Aumakua, spirit of an ancestor; Haikilli, god of thunder; Haumea, goddess of birth; Hina, goddess of moon; Pele, goddess of wind, lightning, and thunder; Nu'u, Hawaiian Noah, and so many more. Your first story is about how Maui, a Polynesian Hero, confronted the sun. Share it with us.

10:04:

Rebecca's First Story: (4–6 minutes max.).

10:10:

Host: Comment. *Question:* "Rebecca, I know Hawaii is influenced by indigenous Polynesian culture as well as Asia. Give us an example of an experience you've had that represents this influence." (Respond in about 30 seconds max.). *Question:* "You've traveled all over Hawaii as an actress and puppeteer performing stories in schools. What sorts of stories did you tell?" (Respond in about 30 seconds max.). Then I will say something like... Rebecca, I want to continue talking about ways stories can instill wisdom right after I remind them that they are enjoying you tell Hawaiian legends on *So, What's Your Story*, on KPFT 90.1, Houston, 89.5 in Galveston, 89.7 in Huntsville, and 90.3 in Livingston. This is your host, Hank Roubicek.

10:12:

Question: "Rebecca, great wisdom is shared through stories from all cultures. In a sentence or two, what is unique about the kind of wisdom conveyed through story?" (Respond in about 30 seconds.). Your next story is a beautiful love story you told at one of our storyteller meetings. Please share it.

10:13:

Rebecca's Second Story: (4–6 minutes max).

10:19:

Host: Comment. *Question:* "You recently returned from Maine where you taught a class in story drama. Tell us about that." (Respond in about 30 seconds.). I will comment, then…This is Hank Roubicek with my guest, Rebecca Narrowe, on *So, What's Your Story?* 90.1, KPFT Houston.

10:21:

Now Tips for the Teller, when we learn something about storytelling from a question asked by one of our listeners. Mickey from Houston asks, "Dr. Hank, it sounds like you love movies because you talk about them often on your show. What's your favorite movie?" Mickey, you're right, I do love movies, and I refer to them on the show because great movies are based on great stories. And the best stories come to life through skillful acting and artful dialogue… without special effects getting in the way. Old movies with a compressed and intense plot: "Casablanca," "Psycho," "12 Angry Men," "The Godfather," "Ordinary People," and in recent years, "The Actor," is a very short list of some of my favorite stories in film form. *Question:* Rebecca, do you have a favorite story told in movie form? Thank you, Mickey.

If you have a question you'd like me to answer on the air or want to be a guest on *So, What's Your Story,* send me your question or story idea to roubey.story@gmail.com (repeat). And I will respond. Our upcoming fall fund drive is around the corner, from October 3–23.

Thanks to you, the last drive was nothing less than spectacular, surpassing our goal for this show by some 600%. Pre-pledges are welcomed and appreciated by going to KPFT.ORG, and leaving a donation for your favorite show, and I hope it's this one. This show, all shows depend on you. My intern and wing-person, Roxy Russell, will be co-hosting during the drive so you'll be meeting her in a couple of weeks.

10:25:

Let me tell you about the Houston Storytellers Guild, of which I am the proud president. Every story lover, from starters to stars belongs in HSG. We hold a monthly Story Swap on the third Tuesday of every month, from 7–8:30 PM, at St. Andrews House, 1811 Heights Blvd. It's a group that rocks! Check out our site at www.houstonstorytellers.org for all the fun happenings.

10:26:

Question: Rebecca, how about another couple of quick Hawaiian anecdotes (Respond in about 30 seconds max.).

10:27:

Music outro about 10:27:55

Rebecca, thank you for your stories, and for the passion with which they were told. This was a fun show. Next week Roxy and I will be asking for your help to keep this show and every show on this freedom-centered, listener-sponsored station. Scooter is next with the Inner Side. Make KPFT a part of every day and make it a habit to tune in every Thursday at 10:00 PM for *So, What's Your Story*, and ease into the weekend right. Be good to each other. I'm Dr. Hank Roubicek always reminding you it's Never Too Late to Live Happily Ever After.

Engineer's Note: 10:28:

Wherever I am, start music softly to cue me a few seconds before 10:27:55. I will shoot for completion by no later than 10:28:30. Raise volume when I'm done and let music roll until 10:29.

Appendix B

To complement traditional storytelling assignments:

I designed this assignment to teach some of the elements of storytelling in a setting other than face-to-face. This can be useful if you are interested in learning how to construct and convey a story program on the radio.

Radio Show Assignment

Time: 6–8 minutes

This assignment is designed to appeal to your creative side, crafted to help you achieve three objectives: (1) display your speech tools (variety of expression, vocal variety, and clear diction); (2) demonstrate the importance of organization and transitions so that messages can be offered to your target audience in guided fashion; and (3) design a focused program on a central theme you make relevant to your audience.

Your programs will be audio recorded in class so you can hear it (and own it) later.

Theme: The theme is defined by the creative message you use to amplify it. For example, you can choose a poem, segment from a prose selection, newspaper article, personal narrative, or the like to communicate your theme. The opening will consist of an attention-getter, designed to convey the relevance of the theme to your target audience (emphasizing the reason they should listen). In the opening, you also introduce yourself, give the name of your program, and convey what you want to accomplish in the next few minutes. Your closing consists of a memorable remark and a gracious exit with appropriate thanks, salutation, and perhaps a sneak preview (teaser) to your next program.

Example

Opening:

Good Morning. I'm Hector Prince with *Morning Thought.* So many of you out there lived through the horrors of the 9/11 tragedy. The notions of heroes were battered about, and ever since that time, we have collectively tried to sort out those attributes of a good hero. So today, I would like to share with you an account of what I think a true hero is by reading this letter (or letters depending on length) written by a young man to his dear wife just minutes before marching into Gettysburg, found in *War Letters*, a series of letters compiled in 2002 by Andrew Carroll of PBS fame.

Read the selection(s)

Closing:

A simple, provocative thought conveyed by this young man. His love for his wife eclipses his obvious youthful naiveté and illiteracy and marks the time in history when love, if you will, is seen to conquer all. He never made it back. He was killed during the first engagement. But for me, the thought worth pondering is how the simplicity of love incarnate is the background and backbone of the true hero. Just something to ponder. Thanks for tuning in. Next week, we will look at the status of online dating—very different from the tender reality of a soldier, his warped, soiled pencil and ragged paper used to send a note to his loving wife. Have a great rest of the morning.

Example

Opening:

This is Harry Peters. Welcome to *Evening Read*. Just the other day, we spent time talking about the most underrated authors of all time, and I asked for you, my insightful listeners, to send in your votes.

Well, we actually have a winner. I received more votes for Edgar Allen Poe than for any other; and after doing a little research, I can understand why he made such an impression on so many of you. To illustrate, he was not a particularly sane man yet convinced his readers otherwise when narrating his self as someone who meticulously chops up a little old man into pieces while proclaiming his sanity in *The Tell Tale Heart*. And "The Raven," for which he received a measly $14.00…a poem with a descriptive prognostication of the death of his beloved wife. I think "The Raven" epitomizes what so many of you find appealing about Poe. Let me read a segment from "The Raven" to make the point.

Read the segment desired

Closing:

"Lenore, Lenore, Never More," echoed endlessly with his signature haunting tone, framed by an eerie but brilliant element no other author has managed to touch. Next week we'll choose another author. In the meantime, keep reading, thinking, sharing, and listening. You've been listening to *Evening Read* with Harry Peters. Good Night.

In a 6–8-minute program, about 70% of your total program should consist of the selection read. So with an 8-minute program, about 6 minutes should center on the reading segment, a 6-minute program about 4 minutes, and so on. It is just an approximation, but your program should not waver much from that formula.

Certainly, use notes. There is no reason to memorize anything. ***However, even with notes in front of you*** (*and full text of your readings*) ***this must be thoroughly rehearsed in order to achieve the learning objectives***. You must KNOW the material and know it well! Also, your program must fall between the 6- and 8-minute range, so you will need to plan your program carefully and thoughtfully.

Appendix C

Some favorite storytelling quotations to ponder . . . & cherish

Stories are often dismissed by "new-agers" as meaningless. They are mentioned as traps of untruth, excuses, or hollow narratives that prevent us from experiencing true happiness in life. This is quite sad, really, because life is happier with stories. Joseph Campbell touted myth as one of the most powerful inventions of humanity, and that our personal stories awaken us to a sense of awe at the mystery of human existence. Stories are beautiful. They may even be the essence of empathy—the key to connecting with others and recognizing our shared experiences. Stories help us to make sense out of the world and, in particular, our own world. For me, rejoicing in the resurgence of storytelling in the twenty-first century world calls for reviving some of the most valued and treasured thoughts tendered by a collection of wise storytellers. For your reflections:

"There is no greater agony than bearing an untold story inside you."
—Maya Angelou

"People are hungry for stories. It's part of our very being. Storytelling is a form of history, of immortality too. It goes from one generation to another."
—Studs Terkel

"Perhaps one day I'll crawl back home, beaten, defeated. But not as long as I can make stories out of my heartbreak, beauty out of sorrow."
—Sylvia Plath

"The destiny of the world is determined less by the battles won than the stories it loves and believes in."
—Harold Goddard

"Nobody has any conscience about adding to the improbabilities of a marvelous tale."
—Nathaniel Hawthorne

"Fantasy is a necessary ingredient in living."
—Dr. Seuss *(Theodor Seuss Geisel)*

"People have forgotten how to tell a story. Stories don't have a middle or an end any more. They usually have a beginning that never stops beginning."
—Steven Spielberg

"Madame, all stories continued long enough end in death, and he is no true storyteller who would keep that from you."
—Ernest Hemingway

"I want a perfect ending. Now I've learned the hard way, that some poems don't rhyme, and some stories don't have a clear beginning, middle, and end. Life is about not knowing, having to change, taking the moment and making the best of it, without knowing what's going to happen next. Delicious Ambiguity."
—Gilda Radner

"I would ask you to remember only this one thing," said Badger. "The stories people tell have a way of taking care of them. If stories come to you, care for them. And learn to give them away where they are needed. Sometimes a person needs a story more than food to stay alive. That is why we put these stories in each other's memory. That is how people care for themselves."
—Barry Lopez

"Faith! He must make his stories shorter or change his comrades once a quarter."
—Jonathon Swift

"It takes a thousand voices to tell a single story."
—Native American saying

"In seeking truth you have to get both sides of the story."
—Walter Cronkite

"Don't say the old lady screamed—bring her on and let her scream."
—Mark Twain

"After nourishment, shelter and companionship, stories are the thing we need most in the world."
—Philip Pullman

"Every great love starts with a great story."
—Nicholas Sparks

"Stories have to be told or they die, and when they die, we can't remember who we are or why we're here."
—Sue Monk Kidd

"A story has no beginning or end: arbitrarily one chooses that moment of experience from which to look back or from which to look ahead."
—Graham Greene

"To hell with facts! We need stories."
—Ken Kesey

"I'll tell you a secret. Old storytellers never die. They disappear in to their own story."
—Vera Nazarian

"Sometimes reality is too complex. Stories give it form."
—Jean–Luc Godard

"The world is shaped by two things—stories told and the memories they leave behind."
—Vera Nazarian

Bibliography

Adams, K. (1990). *Journal to the Self*. New York: Warner Books.

_____. (1994). *Mightier than the Sword* (currently out of print). New York: Warner Books.

Aipes, J. (1994). *The Outspoken Princess and Gentle Knight: A Treasury of Modern Fairy Tales*. New York: Bantam Books.

Akeret, R. (1991). *Family Tales, Family Wisdom*. New York: William Morrow and Company.

Allison, C. (1987). *I'll Tell You a Story, I'll Sing You a Song*. New York: Dell.

Allstrom, E. (1957). *Let's Play a Story*. New York: Friendship Press.

Applebee, A. (1980). *The Child's Concept of Story*. Chicago: The University of Chicago Press.

Baker, A., and Greene, E. (1977). *Storytelling: Art and Technique*. 2nd ed. New York: R.R. Bowker.

Baldwin, C. (2005). *Storycatcher: Making Sense of Our Lives through the Power and Practice of Story*. Novato, CA: New World Library.

Bauer, C. (1993). *New Handbook for Storytellers*. Chicago: American Library Association.

Bettelheim, B. (1975). *The Uses of Enchantment*. New York: Vintage Books.

Blaustein, R. (1989). "A Guide to Collecting Family History and Community Traditions." *Brothers Grimm Newsletter* 2: 4–8.

Blumenthal, M. (2002). *All My Mothers and Fathers: A Memoir*. New York: Harper Collins.

Boas, J., ed. (1996). *We Are Witnesses: Five Diaries of Teenagers Who Died in the Holocaust*. New York: Scholastic Inc.

Bosma, B. (1992). *Fairy Tales, Fables, Legends, and Myths: Using Folk Literature in Your Classroom*. 2nd ed. New York: Teachers College Press.

Briggs, N., and Wagner, J. (1979). *Children's Literature Through Storytelling and Drama*. Dubuque, IA: Wm. C. Brown.

Carroll, A. (2001). *War Letters: Extraordinary Correspondence from American Wars*. New York: Scribner.

Classen, C. (1993). *Worlds of Sense: Exploring the Senses in History and Across Cultures*. New York: Routledge.

Coles, R. (1989). *The Call of Stories: Teaching and the Moral Imagination*. Boston: Houghton Mifflin.

Cooper, P. (1995). *Communication for the Classroom Teacher*. Scottsdale, AZ: Gorsuch Scarisbrick Publishers.

Cooper, P., and Collins, R. (1997). *The Power of Story: Teaching through Storytelling*. Long Grove, IL: Waveland Press, Inc. (reissued)

Dahl, R. (2005). *Collected Stories*. New York: Everyman's Library Publishing.

Ellis, E. (1962). *The Storytelling Framework*. New York: Barnes and Noble, Inc.

_____, and Niemi, L. (2001). *Letting the Wolf In*. Little Rock: August House Publishers.

Farnsworth, K. (1981). "Storytelling in the Classroom." *Language Arts* 58: 162–167.

Fisher, A. (1984). "Narration as a Human Paradigm." *Communication Monographs* 51: 1–22.

_____. (1987). *Human Communication as a Narration: Toward a philosophy of reason, value, and action*. Columbia: SC: University of South Carolina Press.

Frank, Anne. (1947). *The Diary of Anne Frank*. Original publication in the Netherlands.

Heinig, R. (1987). *Creative Drama Resource Book*. Englewood Cliffs, NJ: Prentice-Hall.

Holliday, L. (1995). *Children in the Holocaust and World War II: Their Secret Diaries*. New York: Washington Square Press.

Holmes, N. (1988). "We're All Storytellers." *Learning* 88 17: 82–84.

Holt, D., and Mooney, B., eds. (1994). *Ready-To-Tell Tales: Sure-Fire Stories from America's Favorite Storytellers*. Little Rock: August House.

Izzy, J. B. (2003). *The Beggar King and the Secret of Happiness*. New York: Algonquin Books of Chapel Hill (division of Workman Publishing).

Kalmer, H. (1988). *Communication: Sharing Our Stories of Experience*. Seattle, WA: Psychological Press.

Kingwood, W. (1983). "Storytelling and Self Confrontation: Parables as Communication Strategies." *Quarterly Journal of Speech* 69: 58–74.

Kurtz, E., and Ketchan, K. (2002). *The Spirituality of Imperfection: Storytelling as the Search for Meaning*. New York: Bantam Books.

Lee, H. (1960). *To Kill a Mockingbird*. (40th Anniversary ed., 1999). New York: Harper Collins.

Lenard-Cook, L. (2008). *The Mind of Your Story*. Cincinnati: Writer's Digest Books

Lipman, D. (1999). *Improving Your Storytelling*. Atlanta: August House, Inc.

_____. (1995). *The Storytelling Coach: How to Listen, Praise, and Bring Out People's Best*. Little Rock: August House.

Lopez, B. (1997). *Field Notes: Stories*. Athens, GA: University of Georgia Press.

Loviglio, J. (2005). *Radio's Intimate Public: Network Broadcasting and Mass-Mediated Democracy*. Minneapolis, MN: University of Minnesota Press.

MacDonald, M. (1986). *Twenty Tellable Tales*. New York: H.W. Wilson Publishing.

MacKinlay, E. (1970). *The Shared Experience*. New York: Barnes and Noble, Inc.

Marsden, S. (1980). "Storytellers in the Classroom." *Teacher* 98: 33–36.

McLuhan, M. (2001). *The Medium is the Massage: An Inventory of Effects*. New York: Random House (reissued by Gingko Press).

Medina, E. (1986). "Enhance Your Curriculum Through Storytelling." *Learning* 86 15: 58–61.

Mellon, N. (1998). *Storytelling and the Art of Imagination*. New York: Harper Collins.

Miller, K. (2005). *Communication Theories: Perspectives, processes, and contexts*. New York: McGraw Hill.

Moore, R. (1991). *Awakening the Hidden Storyteller: How to Build a Storytelling Tradition in Your Family*. Springhouse, PA: Shambhala.

O'Callahan, J. (1985). *Master's Class in Storytelling*. Marshfield, MA: Vineyard Productions.

_____. "16 Tips for the Teller." *Teacher* 98: 34–35.

Opie, I., and Opie, P. (1974). *The Classic Fairy Tales*. London: Oxford University Press.

Pellowski, A., and Sweet, L. (1987). *The Family Storytelling Handbook*. New York: Macmillan.

Reinher, R. (1987). "Storytelling." *Teachers and Writers Magazine* 18: 1–7.

Rosenblatt, L., Lakoma, M., and Alexander, V. (2004). "So Short a Lease: Women's Accounts of Living with Advanced Cancer." *Storytelling, Self, Society: An Interdisciplinary Journal of Storytelling Studies* 1: 44–56.

Rossel, S. (2013). *The Wise Folk of Chelm*. Houston: Rossel Books.

Roubicek, H. (1983). "An Investigation of Story Dramatization as a Pre-Writing Activity." Dissertation written at the University of Maryland: College Park, MD.

_____. (1988). "Story Dramatization as a Pedagogical Mechanism for Pre-Writing." Paper presented at the annual meeting of the Speech Communication Association, San Francisco.

Rowland, R. C. (1989). "On Limiting the Narrative Paradigm: three case studies." *Communication Monographs* 56: 39–54.

Sawyer, R. (1998). *The Way of the Storyteller*. New York: Penguin.

Schwartz, M. (1987). "Connecting to Language Through Story." *Language Arts* 64: 603–610.

Seeger, P. (2000). *Pete Seeger's Storytelling Book*. New York: Harcourt Brace.

Seiler, W. J., and Beall, M. (2007). *Communicating: Making Connections*. Boston, MA: Allyn and Bacon.

Shannon, G. (1985). *Stories to Solve*. New York: Greenwillow Books.

Simmons, A., and Philipson, N. (2000). *The Story Factor: Secrets of Influence from the Art of Storytelling*. Cambridge: MA.

Sobol, J. D. (1999). *The Storytellers' Journey: An American Revival*. Urbana, IL: University of Illinois.

Stallings, F. (1988). "The Web of Silence: Storytelling's Power to Hypnotize." *National Storytelling Journal* Spring/Summer: 6–19.

Stone, Richard. (1996). *The Healing Art of Storytelling*. New York: Hyperion Books.

Tatar, M. (editor). (1999). *The Classic Fairy Tales*. New York: W.W. Norton & Company.

Thompson Learning. (1994). *Tales Around the World*. New York: Thompson Learning.

Ward, W. (1958). *Theater for Children*. Anchorage, Kent: Anchorage Press.

Weems, M. L. (1918). *A History of the Life and Death Virtues and Exploits of General George Washington*. Philadelphia: J.B. Lippincott.

Yolen, J. (1986). *Favorite Folktales from Around the World*. New York: Pantheon.

Zinsser, W. (2004). *Writing About Your Life*. Philadelphia: Perseus Books Group.

Zipes, J. (1995). *Creative Storytelling: Building Community, Changing Lives*. New York: Routledge.

Major Storytelling Book Publishers

August House Publishers, Inc.
P.O. Box 3223
Little Rock, AR 72203-3223
www.augusthouse.com

Fulcrum Publishing
350 Indiana Street Suite 350
Golden, CO 80401-5093
www.fulcrum-books.com

Oryx Press
4041 North Central Suite 700
Phoenix, AZ 85012-3397
www.oryxpress.com

H.W. Wilson
950 University Avenue
Bronx, NY 10452
www.hwwilson.com

Yellow Moon Press
P.O. Box 1316
Cambridge, MA 02238
www.yellowmoon.com

Resources

For a full list of *So, What's Your Story?* programs go to
www.houstonstorytellers.org
See "Radio Program" on the left. Click and enjoy.

www.KPFT.ORG
"On Demand" (archives), and scroll to date and program
90.1FM Houston

www.themoth.org/radio

www.thisamericanlife.org

storycorps.org

National Storytelling Network
www.storynet.org
Storytelling Magazine
National Storytelling Network
132 Boone Street Suite 5
Jonesborough, TN 37659
nsn@storynet.org

Lightning Source UK Ltd.
Milton Keynes UK
UKHW022335300819
348844UK00011B/2600/P